I0517782

LAW OF THE LAND

A Practical Legal Guide for Tourists and Business Travelers

Costa Rica

By Michael L. Moore Esq.

Copyright © 2025

Author: Michael L. Moore

Publishing rights reserved worldwide.

All rights reserved as sole property of the author.

The author guarantees all content is original and does not infringe upon the legal rights of any other person or work.

No part of this book may be reproduced, stored in a retrieval system, or transmitted in any form or by any means, without expressed written permission of the author.

Edited by Ally Knez-Siddique

Cover Design: Kristina Conatser

Published by: Law of the Land Publishing LLC

ISBN: 978-1-964870-10-6

DEDICATION

This book is dedicated to the memory of my late older brother, Kenneth Lee Moore, whose tragic murder at 15 years of age inspired me to write this series of books.

This book is also dedicated to my parents, John Henry Moore, and Edna Mae Moore, whose tremendous parenting skills kept me focused on the important things in life: being reverent, getting educated, and prioritizing family.

Finally, this book is dedicated to my beautiful family, my wife Royellen, my son AJ, and my daughter Karla. They inspire me every single day to be kind, patient, and compassionate.

IN LOVING MEMORY OF:

Belinda Joyce Moore Moss—my beautiful and wonderful sister, who supported me in every positive thing that I ever attempted to do.

Michael Eugene Baker—my dedicated and loyal friend and brother, who always wanted the very best for me.

Sylvia Joyce Hill—my eldest sister, who had a beautiful spirit and was like a second mother to me.

LAW OF THE LAND ®
OF THE
PUBLISHING for Tourists & Business Travelers

Travel smart. Stay legal. Stay safe. ®

From local laws to medical guides we've got you covered world wide
in one digital platform.

Travel Safe Anywhere
3 MONTHS FREE TRIAL

SCAN QR code
for more info

PREFACE

My introduction to the justice system came when I was only 10 years old. My 15-year-old brother was murdered with a butcher knife by a 19-year-old in a simple argument over a torn shirt. I was devastated by his death and sought retribution for his fate that never came. The woman was initially charged with second degree murder, but after plea negotiations, she was convicted of manslaughter and sentenced to only five years in a youthful offender school and ordered to undergo psychiatric care. That was it. Nothing more. The judicial system had run its course.

My family knew nothing about the justice system, and we did not have the tools to advocate for ourselves. No one provided us with a written source to reference for guidance through this process. There was no easily accessible, easy to understand, definitive source to educate ourselves about the legal system that we suddenly and unexpectedly found ourselves immersed in after being victimized by such a violent criminal act.

As I got older, finished college, law school, and ultimately started practicing law, it became clear to me that most people are not knowledgeable about the law or how the judicial process works. If most people are uninformed here in the United States regarding the law and the legal process, how would they fare when in other countries? I realized that tourists and businesspeople who travel internationally needed access to information on how to navigate the legal system in other countries!

For many years, there has been considerable media attention focused on international travelers experiencing legal difficulties while traveling abroad. Most of these news stories gained attention in the United States and abroad because they involved American citizens facing punishment that was considered "unconventional" and "harsh" by United States' legal standards. I recall a news story in 1994 regarding Michael Fay, a young American male, who had broken the law in Singapore. He was convicted and sentenced to be caned and or whipped publicly. While the United States Government weighed in on the inappropriate and cruel nature of the punishment, the young American was beaten because he had been convicted under Singapore law.

Similarly, in recent years, international news stories have garnered headlines regarding foreign travelers and their issues with the laws of countries that were not their own. Amanda Knox, an American woman, was accused of murdering her roommate in Italy in 2007 and spent almost four years in an Italian prison before being definitively acquitted by the Supreme Court of Cassatio. Kenneth Bae, an American citizen, was arrested in North Korea in 2012 and was convicted for hostile acts against the communist country. He was sentenced to 15 years hard labor but was released in 2014 after efforts by the U.S. State Department. More recently, United States Basketball Star, Brittany Griner was arrested in February 2022 at a Moscow airport on drug-related charges and detained for nearly 10 months, spending much of that time in prison. Her plight unfolded at the same time Russia invaded Ukraine and further heightened tensions between Russia and the United States, ending only after she was freed in exchange for a notorious Russian arms dealer.

It was in 1994 that another personal tragic event occurred that finally inspired me to write these series of books. A dear friend and also client of mine was brutally murdered while on his second honeymoon in Jamaica. News of his murder shocked me and our local community. The legal hurdles his family had to overcome to see that justice was properly dispensed far away from home, in another country, with an entirely different set of criminal procedural rules and laws, was difficult to navigate.

As I was my friend's attorney at the time of his death, his family asked that I act as their "legal liaison" to the Jamaican Prosecutor's Office and to the Jamaican Police Department. I participated in multiple police interviews with my client's widow because she was the primary witness to his murder. As a former prosecuting attorney, I was also allowed by the Court, as a professional courtesy, to sit at the prosecutor's table to consult with the prosecuting attorney during trial. What I observed about the Jamaican trial process from a front row seat was compelling enough to cause me to seriously consider educating the "world" regarding what to expect and how to act appropriately when faced with legal issues while traveling abroad.

One of the realities in life is that, regardless of what country you are in, it is never a pleasant experience to run afoul of the law and be forced to accept that someone else will be making a decision about your pecuniary, proprietary, or penal interests (your money, your property, or your freedom).

It is important to know what the laws are, how they apply to you, and how to navigate the legal system if you are charged with a crime. It is also very helpful to know what resources are available to you if you are the victim of a criminal act. At the end of the day, an "ounce of prevention is worth a pound of cure," so the more knowledge you have, the more ammunition you possess, and the more likely you will have a positive outcome.

If you are traveling to Costa Rica, the first thing you should pack is a copy of this book! The helpful information and tips contained in this volume will provide a great starting point for knowing what to do (and not to do!) when you arrive at your destination and will help ensure that you have a wonderful vacation or business trip unmarred by tangles with the law.

TABLE OF CONTENTS

INTRODUCTION

INTRODUCTION

As a practicing attorney for over 34 years, I have encountered numerous clients who travel often, but are unaware of the laws of the land they are traveling to.

Therefore, many years ago, I decided to write a series of books that would explain the laws of specific countries. My focus was to explain the laws that may affect travelers in a straightforward manner, without all of the legal language that is sometimes hard for even seasoned attorneys to understand.

About This Book

The aim of this book is simple. It provides you, the traveler, with a simple, easy to read book that will provide a basic legal guide that explains the law in the country that you are about to visit. It is not intended to educate you on ALL of the laws in a given country. The goal is to provide you with the details of the most common legal and safety issues faced by tourists and business travelers.

I have also provided context with background information on places not to visit, statistics on the country and prevention measures you should take to safeguard your legal and physical safety. Knowledge is a powerful thing and knowing how to stay out of trouble (or how to get out of it!) is important for everyone who travels.

This *Law of The Land/Costa Rica* book simply helps you become more informed about your legal rights, responsibilities, and obligations in a wide range of subject areas.

Last, but not least, this book does NOT purport to offer legal advice. It does, however, provide the information you need to stay safe, follow the law and navigate around legal difficulties. However, if you do face legal difficulties, the information in this book will provide you with a starting point for solving the problem and obtaining legal assistance should it be required.

Hypotheticals Used Throughout This Book

From time to time throughout this book, I will explain the law to readers by using hypothetical scenarios. These hypotheticals will be marked by an icon that will be explained in further detail as you read on.

How This Book is Organized

CHAPTER 1: **About Costa Rica.** This chapter will provide you with a brief overview about Costa Rica and its history. It also addresses Visa requirements, monetary advice, and the best times to visit.

CHAPTER 2: **Customs.** This chapter will provide information on what to expect when entering Costa Rica. It will also explain what restricted and prohibited items are when entering Costa Rica along with Customs regulations.

CHAPTER 3: **Crime in Costa Rica.** This chapter provides an overview of the history of crime in Costa Rica and steps that Costa Rican officials have taken to curb the high rate of crime.

CHAPTER 4: **Criminal Law Violations.** This chapter will provide information on drug offenses, penalties, true events and questions and answers.

CHAPTER 5: **Alcohol-Related Offenses.** This chapter will provide key points regarding the sale, consumption, and regulations of alcohol use in Costa Rica.

CHAPTER 6: **Firearm & Ammunition Offenses.** This chapter will provide key points regarding the possession of firearms and ammunition in Costa Rica.

CHAPTER 7: **Prostitution.** This chapter provides an overview of the history of prostitution in Costa Rica, laws and penalties, prostitution practices, sex trafficking, sex tourism, and health in Costa Rica, tips to avoid being hassled, a Law of the Land Hypothetical and the current situation on prostitution in Costa Rica.

CHAPTER 8: **LGBTQ.** This chapter will provide information regarding the acceptance of LGBTQ people in Costa Rica, and the laws surrounding homosexuality.

CHAPTER 9: **Sexually Motivated/Violent Crimes.** This chapter will provide an overview of sexually related crimes in Costa Rica.

CHAPTER 10: **Arrested in Costa Rica.** This chapter will provide information on what to do if you are arrested in Costa Rica.

CHAPTER 11: **Jails vs. Prisons: Conditions & Culture.** This chapter will provide information on the conditions and culture of Costa Rican Jails and Prisons.

CHAPTER 12: **Helping a Friend or Relative Imprisoned in Costa Rica.** This chapter will provide information on how you can assist a friend or relative imprisoned in Costa Rica.

CHAPTER 13: **The Administration of Justice.** This chapter will provide information on Costa Rica's Legal System.

CHAPTER 14: **Crime Victim Assistance.** This chapter will provide information on crime victim assistance along with providing safety tips.

CHAPTER 15: **Police.** This chapter will provide information on the Costa Rican Police and how to report a crime.

CHAPTER 16: **How to Get Legal Help in Costa Rica.** This chapter will provide information regarding how to obtain legal assistance for travelers to Costa Rica.

CHAPTER 17: **Medical Facilities & Hospitals.** This chapter will provide information about how to obtain medical care while visiting Costa Rica.

CHAPTER 18: **Driving in Costa Rica.** This chapter will provide information on Driving in Costa Rica, it's Traffic Rules, and Road Safety Tips.

CHAPTER 19: **Nude Beaches and Clothing-Optional Resorts.** This chapter will provide an overview of nude beaches and clothing-optional resorts in Costa Rica, and the legality and safety of visiting nude beaches in Costa Rica.

CHAPTER 20: **Unusual Laws.** This chapter will provide information on some Unusual Laws in Costa Rica, and penalties and fines.

CHAPTER 21: **Traveling Safely.** This chapter will provide information on women traveling alone, crime prevention for families, safety notes for all travelers, and overall advice.

CHAPTER 22: **Tourist Taxation.** This chapter will provide information on taxes that tourists are required to pay in Costa Rica.

CHAPTER 23: **Long-Term Stays.** This chapter will provide an overview of the consequences for overstaying your visit to Costa Rica.

CHAPTER 24: **Civil Litigation.** This chapter will provide information about the civil litigation process in Costa Rica.

CHAPTER 25: **Other Things to Know.** This chapter will provide information on the harassment of tourists, travel and safety, and other practical tips.

CHAPTER 26: **Quick Reference Guide.** This chapter is a quick way to get information. It is a condensed version of the chapters in this book.

Emergency/Important Contact Numbers in Costa Rica

Useful Spanish Phrases

Glossary

Icons Used in this Book

What do those pictures throughout the book mean? See below:

 WARNING: This icon flags information about things you should **avoid** while visiting Costa Rica. Heed the advice next to this icon to avoid legal perils.

 REMEMBER: This icon flags noteworthy information that you **shouldn't forget**.

 HELPFUL TIPS: This icon flags information that will help you when entering Costa Rica, relates to a legal situation, or refers to resources available while visiting Costa Rica.

 TECHNICAL INFORMATION: This icon flags technical aspects of the law. If you are faced with a legal problem, and you want to learn more about the law involved, this information can be helpful.

ADDITIONAL INFORMATION: This icon points to the location of additional information available on the internet.

HYPOTHETICAL: This icon points to hypothetical scenarios to illustrate possible legal problems and the outcome.

QUESTIONS: This icon points to questions and answers throughout the book.

TRUE STORY: This icon points to true events throughout the book.

Where to Go From Here

If you have a specific question about the law in Costa Rica as it relates to a particular area, just turn to the chapter that addresses that issue, or turn to the Quick Reference Guide. You can also read the book from cover to cover to obtain a more comprehensive understanding of the Costa Rican laws and resources available should you find yourself in a legal predicament while visiting.

Disclaimer: While the recommendations in this book primarily address U.S. citizens, the information is relevant and applicable to citizens of any country.

ABOUT COSTA RICA

- About Costa Rica
- Costa Rica, the Basics
- Costa Rican Hospitality

ABOUT COSTA RICA

About Costa Rica

Costa Rica is located in Central America, bordered by Nicaragua to the north, Panama to the southeast, the Pacific Ocean to the west, and the Caribbean Sea to the east. Its geographical position places it between two major oceans, making it a prime destination for biodiversity and eco-tourism.

Costa Rica has an area of approximately **51,100 square kilometers** (19,700 square miles). This makes it slightly smaller than West Virginia in the United States but rich in diverse ecosystems despite its size.

As of the most recent estimates (2023), Costa Rica has a population of around **5.4 million people.** The population density varies, with most people living in the central and western regions of the country, particularly around the capital, San José.

Costa Rica's history dates back to pre-Columbian times, when it was inhabited by various indigenous groups such as the Chorotega, Bribri, and Cabécar. The Spanish arrived in the early 1500s, led by Juan de Cavallón, and Costa Rica became part of the Spanish Empire. It was not seen as a lucrative colony, which led to its relatively slow development compared to other regions of Latin America. After gaining independence from Spain in 1821, Costa Rica briefly became part of the Mexican Empire and then the United Provinces of Central America, before becoming a fully independent republic in 1838. Throughout the 19th and 20th centuries, Costa Rica developed a stable political system, becoming known for its strong democracy, abolition of the army in 1949, and a focus on education, health, and environmental conservation.

Today, Costa Rica is known for its rich biodiversity, eco-tourism, and commitment to environmental sustainability. It boasts an impressive array of national parks and protected areas, making it a top destination for nature lovers and adventure seekers. The country is also famous for its "Pura Vida" lifestyle, emphasizing happiness, well-being, and a laid-back approach to life. Additionally, Costa Rica is recognized for its political stability, high standard of living, and being one of the few countries in the world to have abolished its military.

The Capital

The capital of Costa Rica is **San José**, located in the central valley of the country. As the largest city, it serves as the political, economic, and cultural hub of Costa Rica. San José is home to government buildings, museums, theaters, and historical landmarks, reflecting the country's rich heritage. The city has a lively atmosphere with a mix of colonial architecture and modern development. While it is often seen as a starting point for travelers heading to the country's natural wonders, San José offers its own attractions, including vibrant markets, art galleries, and bustling street life. Despite being a busy urban center, it is surrounded by mountains and volcanoes, offering beautiful views and a pleasant climate.

The People

The people of Costa Rica, known as **Ticos** (a term of endearment derived from their tendency to add "-tico" to words), are renowned for their warmth, friendliness, and laid-back attitude. Family-oriented and community-driven, Costa Ricans place a strong emphasis on social well-being and a high quality of life. Costa Rica has a diverse population, primarily of mestizo (mixed Indigenous and European descent), with smaller Afro-Costa Rican, Indigenous, and European communities. Costa Ricans are proud of their country's democratic values, political stability, and commitment to peace, particularly its decision to abolish the military in 1949. A strong national identity is also shaped by the country's motto, "Pura Vida," which reflects their optimistic and relaxed approach to life. Costa Ricans value education, healthcare, and environmental preservation, making them one of the happiest populations in the world.

Language

The official language of Costa Rica is **Spanish**, spoken by the vast majority of the population. Costa Rican Spanish has a distinct, gentle accent and includes local expressions and slang, such as the famous phrase "Pura Vida." While Spanish is dominant, English is widely understood, especially in tourist areas, as many Costa Ricans are bilingual due to the country's strong ties to the global community and its focus on tourism. In addition, some Indigenous groups in Costa Rica, such as the Bribri and Cabécar, continue to speak their native languages, though these are less commonly heard in urban areas.

Religion

Costa Rica is predominantly **Roman Catholic**, with about 60-70% of the population identifying as Catholic. The country has a strong Catholic heritage, reflected in its many churches, religious festivals, and traditions. However, in recent decades, there has been a noticeable increase in **Evangelical Protestant** communities, which now make up around 15-20% of the population. Religious freedom is guaranteed by the Constitution, and while Catholicism holds cultural significance, Costa Rica is a pluralistic society with a growing number of people identifying as secular or unaffiliated with any religion. Despite this diversity, religion plays an important role in Costa Rican life, with many major holidays tied to religious observance.

Affordability

Costa Rica is generally considered affordable, though the cost of living and visiting can vary depending on location and lifestyle. For those living in the country, housing, food, and healthcare are relatively inexpensive, especially outside major cities or popular tourist destinations. Rural areas or smaller towns tend to offer lower living costs, with rent for basic accommodations ranging from US$300 to $600 a month. Local produce and healthcare are also affordable, making it a popular choice for expats and retirees. However, costs can rise in urban centers like San José or beach towns, where demand for housing and services is higher.

For travelers, Costa Rica offers a wide range of options. Budget travelers can enjoy the country for around US$30 to $50 per day, staying in hostels or guesthouses and eating at local sodas (small eateries). Those with a mid-range budget will likely spend between US$100 to $150 per day, enjoying comfortable accommodations, tours, and meals at mid-range restaurants. For luxury travelers, costs can increase significantly, especially in upscale resorts or private tours.

Costa Rica, the Basics

How to Get There?

Costa Rica is well-connected internationally, with several major airports serving as entry points for travelers. The two primary international airports are:

1. **Juan Santamaría International Airport** (SJO). Located near the capital, San José, SJO is the busiest airport in the country and serves as the main gateway for most international flights. It handles flights from North America, Europe, and other parts of Latin America.

2. **Daniel Oduber Quirós International Airport** (LIR). Situated in Liberia, on the Pacific coast, LIR is the second-largest airport, primarily serving visitors flying in from North America and other international destinations, particularly those heading to the beach regions.

Costa Rica is served by a wide range of international airlines, including both major carriers and low-cost options. Some of the airlines that fly to and from Costa Rica include:

- American Airlines
- Delta Air Lines
- United Airlines
- JetBlue Airways
- Copa Airlines
- Spirit Airlines
- Aeromexico
- Air Canada
- Iberia (for European flights)

These airlines provide direct flights to Costa Rica from major cities across the U.S., Canada, and Europe, with additional connections from Central and South America.

The **cheapest times to fly** to Costa Rica are typically during the green season, which runs from **May to November**. This period coincides with the rainy season, which means fewer tourists, lower prices for flights, accommodations, and tours. However, the rain is often concentrated in the afternoons, leaving plenty of sunshine for outdoor activities. The **high season**, from **December to April**, is Costa Rica's dry season and also the most expensive time to visit. During this period, flights, hotels, and tours tend to be more expensive due to the influx of tourists.

For the best deals, it's advisable to book your flights well in advance and consider traveling during shoulder seasons, such as April or November, when the weather is still favorable, but prices are somewhat lower.

When to Visit?

The best time to visit Costa Rica largely depends on what you're looking for in terms of weather, crowds, and activities.

Generally speaking, the best time to visit Costa Rica is during the **dry season** from **December to April**, when the weather is sunny, warm, and ideal for beach activities, hiking, and exploring the country's national parks. This period, however, is also the peak tourist season, so expect larger crowds and higher prices. For a quieter, more affordable experience, the **rainy season** from **May to November** offers lush landscapes and fewer tourists, though rain typically falls in the afternoons, leaving mornings for outdoor activities. The rainy season is great for nature lovers, wildlife enthusiasts, and those seeking a more peaceful visit.

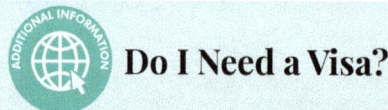 ## Do I Need a Visa?

Whether you need a visa to visit Costa Rica depends on your nationality and the purpose of your visit.

For most travelers, tourist visas are not required for short visits (typically up to 90 days) if you are from a country that has a visa-exempt agreement with Costa Rica. This includes citizens from the United States, Canada, European Union countries, Australia, and many Latin American countries. In these cases, you can enter Costa Rica with just your valid passport.

Citizens of some countries, especially those with limited visa-exempt agreements with Costa Rica, will need to apply for a visa before entering. You can check with the Costa Rican consulate or embassy in your country to determine whether a visa is required.

If you're planning to stay longer than 90 days or if you plan to work or study, you may need a specific visa or permit. Make sure your passport is valid for at least six months from the date of entry into Costa Rica. Also keep in mind that, depending on your nationality, you may need to show proof of onward travel (like a return ticket) upon arrival. To avoid surprises, it's always a good idea to verify visa requirements with your local Costa Rican embassy or consulate before your trip.

How to Get Around

Getting around Costa Rica is relatively easy for tourists, with several convenient options depending on your itinerary and budget. Renting a car offers flexibility and is ideal for exploring remote areas, though **4x4 vehicles** are recommended for rugged terrain. For a hassle-free experience, **private transfers** or **shared shuttles** are great, especially for traveling between popular destinations like San José and Manuel Antonio.

If you're on a budget, the **public bus system** is extensive and affordable, though travel times can be long, and buses may not be as comfortable. **Domestic flights** are available for covering longer distances quickly, particularly between popular tourist spots. In cities like San José, **taxis** and **Uber** are reliable and convenient for short trips. For a more active option, **biking** is available in some tourist areas, and **boats** or **water taxis** are essential for traveling to islands or certain coastal regions. The best option depends on your travel style, destination, and budget.

 **Monetary Advice**

The official currency of Costa Rica is the Costa Rican Colón ₡ (CRC). As of recent exchange rates, US$1 (USD) is roughly equivalent to ₡550-600, though this can fluctuate. It's a good idea to check the current exchange rate before exchanging money. The Colón is used for all transactions, but US dollars are widely accepted, especially in tourist areas, hotels, and larger businesses. When paying in dollars, you may receive change in colones, so it's helpful to carry some local currency as well for smaller purchases.

Credit cards, particularly Visa and MasterCard, are widely accepted in Costa Rica, especially in tourist areas, hotels, restaurants, and larger stores. However, smaller businesses, rural areas, or certain tours may only accept cash, so it's always a good idea to carry some colones on hand. ATMs are widely available, and you can withdraw both colones and dollars using your international debit or credit card. Keep in mind that some ATMs charge fees for withdrawals, and there may be limits on how much you can take out per day. When using US dollars, most establishments will accept them at roughly the current exchange rate, but you may get a slightly less favorable rate than what you would get at a currency exchange.

Bargaining

Bargaining is generally **not common** in Costa Rica, especially in established stores, restaurants, or tourist areas where prices are fixed. However, in local markets (such as artisan markets or roadside stands), some haggling may be possible, particularly when buying in bulk or larger items. In these situations, it's important to be polite and respectful when negotiating prices. For the most part, though, prices are fairly set, and locals usually don't expect extensive bargaining.

Tipping

Tipping in Costa Rica is appreciated but not mandatory. In restaurants, a **10% service charge** is often included in the bill, but an additional tip of **5-10%** is common for excellent service.

For **taxis**, rounding up the fare or leaving **10-15%** is customary. In **hotels**, tipping **US$1-2** per night for housekeeping or bellhops is appreciated, and for **tour guides**, a tip of **US$5-10** per person for half-day tours is typical. While not required, tipping for good service is always welcomed.

Costa Rican Hospitality

Costa Rica is famous for its warm, welcoming hospitality. The people, known as Ticos, are friendly and laid-back, often going out of their way to make visitors feel at home. The phrase *"Pura Vida,"* meaning "pure life" or "full of life," reflects this positive and welcoming attitude. Ticos express their hospitality by showing genuine interest in others, offering help, and inviting visitors to join meals or activities. **Politeness** is important, and simple gestures like saying *"por favor"* (please) and *"gracias"* (thank you) are highly appreciated. Handshakes are common for formal greetings, but in more relaxed settings, especially in rural areas, a hug or kiss on the cheek may be used.

Respect is key in Costa Rican culture. It is polite to greet people, even strangers, and modesty is valued, so avoid boasting or being overly critical. Being punctual is appreciated, although a slight delay is not considered rude in rural areas. Interrupting others or raising your voice can be seen as impolite, and it's best to avoid sensitive topics like politics or religion unless you're well-acquainted with the person. To show respect as a visitor, embrace local customs and try speaking a few words in Spanish. Respecting the environment is also important, as Costa Rica is committed to sustainability—avoid littering or damaging nature. When invited into a home, a small gift like wine or local treats is a thoughtful gesture. Dress modestly, especially in religious settings, and be patient, as Costa Ricans have a relaxed pace of life. By following these customs, you'll foster positive connections and enjoy a richer experience in Costa Rica.

CUSTOMS

- Travelers Entering Costa Rica
- Customs Entitlements and Monetary Restrictions
- Restricted and Prohibited Items
- Five Practical Tips to Know Before You Go

CHAPTER 2

CUSTOMS

Travelers Entering Costa Rica

To enter Costa Rica, travelers typically need the following documents and meet certain requirements:

1. **Valid Passport:** Your passport must be valid for at least 6 months from your planned date of entry into Costa Rica. This applies to most international travelers.

2. **Return or Onward Ticket:** Costa Rican authorities may require proof of onward travel, such as a return flight ticket or a ticket to another destination. This shows that you intend to leave the country within the allowed time frame (usually 90 days for most tourists).

3. **Tourist Visa (If Applicable):** Citizens from certain countries may need to obtain a visa before traveling to Costa Rica. Citizens from many countries, such as the United States, Canada, and most European Union nations, do not require a visa for stays of up to 90 days. However, if you're from a country with visa restrictions, you may need to apply for a visa in advance at a Costa Rican embassy or consulate.

4. **Proof of Sufficient Funds:** In some cases, travelers may need to show proof of sufficient funds to cover their stay. This could be in the form of bank statements, credit cards, or other evidence of financial means.

5. **Vaccination Requirements:** As of now, Costa Rica does not require vaccinations for entry, but it's always good practice to be up to date on routine vaccinations. However, yellow fever vaccination is required for travelers coming from countries with a risk of yellow fever transmission, such as certain areas of South America and Africa.

6. **Tourist Card:** Some travelers may be required to pay for a tourist card upon entry (typically for visitors traveling by air). This is a small fee that helps fund the country's tourism and immigration services. It is sometimes included in your airfare if you're flying to Costa Rica.

7. **Health Insurance:** While not always mandatory, some travelers may be asked to show proof of health insurance coverage during their stay. This is particularly relevant in the case of unforeseen medical emergencies. Costa Rica's Tourist Health Insurance is an option for travelers, especially in the wake of the COVID-19 pandemic.

It's always a good idea to verify entry requirements with the Costa Rican consulate or embassy in your country, as requirements can change. Make sure your documents are in order well in advance of your trip.

When you land in Costa Rica, the arrival process is straightforward. After disembarking, you'll go through immigration, presenting your passport and possibly a return or onward ticket. Be ready to answer questions about your stay and have any required documents, like proof of sufficient funds or a visa, if necessary. Once through, you'll collect your luggage and pass through customs. Costa Rica has relaxed customs checks, but you must declare restricted items like fresh produce or meats.

Currency exchange booths and ATMs are available, though US dollars are widely accepted. You'll find transportation options like official taxis, private shuttles, and car rental desks at the airport. While there's no arrival tax, a departure tax may apply, often included in your airfare.

Costa Rican airports are modern and welcoming, with a friendly "Pura Vida" atmosphere, but always watch your belongings. Lastly, while COVID-19 restrictions have been lifted, check any health or entry requirements before traveling. Overall, the process is smooth, and with a bit of preparation, you'll be ready to begin your adventure in Costa Rica.

Customs Entitlements and Monetary Restrictions[1]

Costa Rica does not impose strict limits on the amount of foreign currency you can bring into the country. However, if you are carrying more than US$10,000 (or its equivalent in other currencies), you must declare it at customs. This is in line with international anti-money laundering regulations.

Generally, items for personal use such as clothing, toiletries, electronics, and souvenirs are allowed without issue. However, if you're carrying high-value items (e.g., electronics), it's a good idea to declare them to avoid complications if you're asked.

You are allowed to bring two bottles of alcohol (liquor, wine, or beer) for personal consumption. Larger quantities may raise suspicion and may be subject to duties or additional inspection.

You can bring in up to 200 cigarettes or 50 cigars for personal use, or 250 grams (8.8 ounces) of tobacco.

If you're arriving at the airport after international travel, you can buy items like alcohol, perfume, and cigarettes from duty-free shops. These purchases are generally allowed without any further tax or duty, as long as you stay within the personal-use limits.

 ## Restricted and Prohibited Items

Certain items are either prohibited or restricted from being imported into Costa Rica.

---

1   https://www.worldbaggagenetwork.com/kb/
     costa-rica/2-customs-regulations-costa-rica

Costa Rica is very strict about the importation of fresh fruits, vegetables, and plants. These are restricted to prevent the introduction of pests and diseases that could harm the local agriculture. Avoid bringing in any fresh food, seeds, or soil unless you have prior permission.

The importation of meats, dairy products, and certain animal products is also highly regulated. Bringing in these items without declaration may lead to confiscation. If you plan to carry these items, check with Costa Rican authorities about any special permits.

Prohibited items further include:

- Illegal drugs and controlled substances. Costa Rica has stringent drug laws, and penalties for violating these can be severe.

- Firearms and ammunition. Visitors wishing to bring a firearm into the country must obtain special permits in advance (discussed in Chapter 6).

- Items made from endangered species, such as certain types of coral, turtle shells, or ivory. These are protected under international conventions and Costa Rican law.

- Fireworks or explosives without proper permits.

Bringing restricted or prohibited items into Costa Rica can lead to serious consequences, including the confiscation of the goods, fines, or even legal action in the case of illegal substances, weapons, or endangered species products. In some cases, such as with illegal drugs or large quantities of controlled items, travelers may face criminal charges, detention, or deportation. Items like fresh produce and meats that are prohibited are typically seized and disposed of. Additionally, failure to declare restricted goods can result in delays and extended inspections at customs. To avoid these issues, it's essential to be aware of and adhere to Costa Rica's customs regulations, declaring any potentially restricted items upon arrival.

For a more detailed list on restricted and prohibited items when traveling to Costa Rica, please visit **https://www. trade.gov/country-commercial-guides/ costa-rica-prohibited-and-restricted-imports**.

Five Practical Tips to Know Before You Go

1. **Learn Basic Spanish Phrases:** While many Costa Ricans speak English, especially in tourist areas, learning a few basic Spanish phrases like "*Hola*" (hello), "*Gracias*" (thank you), and "*Por favor*" (please) will go a long way. Costa Ricans, or "Ticos," appreciate when visitors make an effort to speak their language, and it can help you in rural areas where English is less common.

2. **Pack Light and Smart:** Costa Rica's climate varies by region, but it's mostly warm and tropical. If you're visiting the rainforests or beach towns, lightweight clothing, comfortable shoes, and a rain jacket are a must. For more mountainous areas, bring a light sweater or jacket as temperatures can be cooler. Don't forget insect repellent for the rainforests, and a waterproof bag for your electronics.

3. **Get Travel Insurance:** It's always a good idea to have travel insurance, especially when engaging in adventure activities like zip-lining, surfing, or hiking. Costa Rica's medical care is excellent, but you may still need insurance for unexpected medical expenses or trip disruptions.

4. **Plan Your Transportation:** Costa Rica's public transportation system is reliable but not always convenient for tourists. Renting a car or booking a shuttle service can make your travels easier, especially if you're venturing outside the main cities. Keep in mind that roads can be bumpy and difficult, especially in rural areas or during the rainy season.

5. **Know the Entry Requirements:** Make sure your passport is valid for at least 6 months beyond your travel date, and if required, check whether you need a visa or tourist card. Additionally, some travelers may need to show proof of health insurance upon arrival, depending on current regulations.

CRIME IN COSTA RICA

- Overview
- Crime Hotspots in Costa Rica
- Crime Statistics
- Quick Safety Tips

CRIME IN COSTA RICA

Overview

Costa Rica is generally considered a **safe** destination for tourists compared to many other Central American countries. Most visitors experience little to no issues, and violent crime is relatively rare, especially when compared to neighboring nations. However, like any popular travel spot, Costa Rica is not immune to crime. Petty crime, particularly **theft** and **pickpocketing**, can be a concern in more crowded, tourist-heavy areas such as San José, Jaco, and Puerto Viejo. These types of crimes are typically opportunistic, with criminals taking advantage of distracted tourists in busy places like markets, beaches, or public transport.

The factors contributing to crime in Costa Rica largely stem from socio-economic issues. While the country enjoys a higher standard of living compared to some of its neighbors, **poverty** and **unemployment** in certain regions can drive property crime. Despite violent crime remaining relatively low, there has been a rise in **drug-related violence** and **gang activity**, mainly in coastal and border regions since Costa Rica serves as a transit country for drug trafficking. However, these incidents are generally not aimed at tourists and are more likely to affect those involved in the drug trade or organized crime.

Tourism itself can also play a role in crime. The influx of visitors each year attracts criminals looking to take advantage of unattended valuables or distracted tourists, but violent incidents involving tourists are rare. Most crimes are non-violent and involve **scams** or **theft**. Though Costa Rica's police force is generally reliable, there are areas where **corruption** or inefficiencies can hinder crime prevention efforts, especially in certain urban areas.

Crime Hotspots in Costa Rica

While Costa Rica as a whole may still exude charm and allure, certain areas have become notorious for high crime rates. According to reports from the U.S. Embassy, regions such as San José, Jacó, and Manuel Antonio have seen a significant uptick in crime, particularly robberies and drug-related incidents.[2] In particular, the district of **Jacó de Garabito** recorded the highest rate of crimes against foreign tourists from 2021 to 2023, indicating a stark warning to potential visitors.[3]

San José, the capital city, continues to experience high crime rates, particularly in neighborhoods such as Coca-Cola and Pavas, which are more prone to pickpocketing, robberies, and scams, particularly in busy spots like markets and public transportation hubs. Gang activity can also be found in some parts of the city. While San José has many safe areas, it's advisable to exercise caution, especially at night.

The popular beach town of **Jaco** on the Pacific coast has seen an uptick in crime, primarily theft and drug-related offenses as well. While it remains a major tourist hub, the area can attract opportunistic criminals targeting visitors' belongings, especially on the beach or in rented cars.

Another beach town popular with tourists, **Puerto Viejo** also faces issues with drug trafficking and petty crime. Theft from hotels, cars, and personal belongings is not uncommon. While Puerto Viejo has a laid-back atmosphere, it's still wise to stay alert, particularly after dark.

---

2   https://ticotimes.net/2024/12/25/
    costa-rica-travel-safety-alert-tourist-areas-report-rising-crime-rates

3   https://cronkitenews.azpbs.org/2024/10/18/
    costa-rica-face-record-breaking-levels-crime-tourists

Liberia, the gateway to Costa Rica's Guanacaste province and nearby beaches, has had increased reports of robbery and drug-related crimes. The city's proximity to major transportation routes and its role as a trade and tourism hub can make it a hotspot for opportunistic crime, particularly around the bus stations and tourist areas.

Both the northern and southern **Pacific coastlines**, particularly around **Quepos**, **Manuel Antonio**, and **Nosara**, are known for drug trafficking and occasional gang violence, though these incidents are usually not directed at tourists. However, petty crime can occur in tourist-heavy areas, including theft from vehicles and hotels.

Travel advisory websites provide critical insights into crime-prone regions. For instance, the U.S. State Department advises tourists to exercise heightened caution in many parts of Costa Rica, especially in areas frequented by tourists due to increasing incidents of robbery and violence. Similarly, the Canadian government cautions visitors about prevalent petty crimes and the potential for violent clashes in zones like San José and coastal tourist areas.

For more information on what areas to avoid when traveling to Costa Rica, please visit **https://travel.state. gov/content/travel/en/traveladvisories/traveladvisories/costa-rica-travel-advisory.html**.

Crime Statistics

When compared to **global crime averages**, Costa Rica's **violent crime rate** is relatively low. For instance, as of 2023, Costa Rica's homicide rate stands at 17.3 per 100,000 inhabitants, which is comparatively high when contrasted with the United States, where the same metric is approximately 7.8 per 100,000, but much lower than some of its Central

American neighbors, such as El Salvador and Honduras (which has one of the highest murder rates in the world).[4]

In terms of **petty crime**, Costa Rica's rate is **higher** than in many Western countries, but still below more crime-heavy regions in Latin America. For example, Mexico and Brazil have higher rates of street crime and armed robberies in tourist areas. Costa Rica's overall crime levels, particularly violent crime, are still lower than many countries with similar levels of tourism.

Costa Rica's law enforcement system is generally considered effective in maintaining public order, especially in tourist areas. The country benefits from a long-standing tradition of political stability and civilian policing, having abolished its military in 1948. This has allowed resources to be focused on police forces and education. However, the police force is not without challenges, a problem that will be discussed in Chapter 15. The **National Police** and **Tourism Police** in Costa Rica generally make strong efforts to curb crime in tourist-heavy areas, though they are sometimes criticized for not having sufficient presence in smaller or off-the-beaten-path areas, where petty crime can go unchecked.

It's important to note that while Costa Rica is relatively safe compared to its regional counterparts, the rising popularity of the country as a tourist destination has made it a target for more opportunistic crimes, and so the tourists need to stay well informed and vigilant when traveling to Costa Rica.

---

4   https://www.internationalcitizens.com/blog/expatriate-living/costa-rica-safe.php

Quick Safety Tips

To stay safe, U.S. citizens are advised to exercise heightened vigilance. Protective measures include keeping passports and valuables secured in a hotel safe, avoiding areas with high concentrations of bars and nightclubs, and staying alert in crowded or deserted places. When using transportation, it's important to lock car doors, keep valuables out of sight, and only use licensed taxis. Additionally, travelers should be cautious with financial transactions, change money at reputable institutions, and regularly monitor bank accounts for fraud. Traveling in groups, avoiding physical confrontations, and reporting suspicious activity to the police can also reduce risk.[5]

---

5   https://cr.usembassy.gov/services/threat-from-crime/

CRIMINAL LAW VIOLATIONS

CRIMINAL LAW VIOLATIONS

Marijuana and Other Drugs in Costa Rica

Costa Rica has a complicated history with cannabis and other drugs, shaped by shifting societal views and changing laws. While marijuana has traditionally been illegal, the country's stance on cannabis is evolving, particularly in terms of its medical use.

The presence of cannabis in Costa Rica dates back to the late 19th century when it entered the country through laborers associated with the United Fruit Company. Initially, cannabis was used primarily for agricultural purposes; however, societal attitudes began to shift as Western cultural influences and countercultures propagated its recreational use. The formal illegalization of cannabis came in 1928, which marked the beginning of a contentious relationship between the people and the substance.[6]

Throughout the 20th century, the perception of cannabis continued to evolve alongside changing attitudes towards drug use globally. The U.S. pushed for stringent anti-drug policies, and Costa Rica was not immune to these pressures, adopting some of the strict cannabis laws seen in its northern neighbor. By 1961, Costa Rica had aligned with international

---

6   https://digitalcommons.humboldt.edu/etd/704

prohibitive norms set forth by the United Nations, embedding cannabis prohibition within its legal framework through the General Health
Law.[7]

In recent years, the perceptions around cannabis have softened significantly, mirroring global trends toward decriminalization and legalization. The movement towards cannabis reform began to gain traction
in the early 21st century, influenced by studies highlighting potential
medical benefits and a cultural shift prioritizing personal freedoms. In
March **2022**, Costa Rica took a significant step by **legalizing medical
marijuana**, a reflection of evolving attitudes towards cannabis and its
potential therapeutic uses.[8]

However, the use of **recreational marijuana** remains **illegal** in Costa
Rica. Although there have been public debates about decriminalizing or
legalizing recreational cannabis, there has been no significant movement
toward full legalization yet. Cannabis is still classified as a controlled
substance, and possession of even small amounts can lead to fines or
imprisonment.

In 2022, there were public discussions on the possibility of legalizing
recreational marijuana to boost the economy and regulate the market,
but the legal environment has not yet changed in a substantial way.
Some lawmakers have called for the decriminalization of personal cannabis use, but as of now, recreational use remains outside the bounds of
legality.

Synthetic Cannabinoids

Synthetic cannabinoids—which are lab-made substances designed to
mimic the effects of natural cannabis—are **illegal** in Costa Rica. These
drugs are part of the broader category of designer drugs, and their use,
possession, and distribution are prohibited under Costa Rican drug

---

7   https://thecostaricanews.com/
    marijuana-in-costa-rica-laws-history-and-potential/

8   https://mjbizdaily.com/
    costa-rica-issues-first-medical-marijuana-cultivation-license/

laws. Unlike natural cannabis, synthetic cannabinoids can have highly unpredictable and dangerous effects, leading to serious health risks.

As such, Costa Rican authorities have enforced a strict ban on these substances. There is no official, separate law specifically targeting synthetic cannabinoids, but they fall under the broader Narcotic Drugs Law, which criminalizes the use, possession, trafficking, and production of illegal drugs. Individuals caught with synthetic cannabinoids can face similar penalties to those caught with marijuana or other illegal drugs, including fines and imprisonment.

Other Illegal Drugs[9]

Costa Rica's drug laws are quite strict, and while marijuana has seen some loosening in terms of medical use, other drugs—including **cocaine, methamphetamines, heroin**, and **ecstasy**—are illegal, and the laws surrounding them are harsh.

Costa Rica is a major transit point for cocaine trafficking due to its location between Colombia and North America, but possession and trafficking of **cocaine** are **illegal**. Costa Rica has some of the toughest penalties in the region for drug trafficking, which can include long prison sentences and heavy fines. Possession of small amounts can lead to imprisonment, and drug-related offenses are treated severely by the legal system.

Both **methamphetamines** and **heroin** are classified as **illegal narcotics**, and their production, sale, and possession are punishable under Costa Rican law. The country has not seen as much of a methamphetamine problem as in other parts of the world, but these drugs are still considered dangerous, and law enforcement takes a strong stance against their use.

Ecstasy (MDMA), **LSD**, and other **club drugs** are **illegal** in Costa Rica. Although these drugs are more commonly used in certain tourist party areas, particularly near beaches and in major cities, possession or use

9   https://maint.loc.gov/law/help/decriminalization-of-narcotics/costarica.php

remains illegal. As with other illicit drugs, those caught with ecstasy or similar substances can face criminal charges, including imprisonment.

Prescription drugs, including certain **opioids** and **benzodiazepines**, are **tightly controlled** in Costa Rica. Possession of large quantities of prescription medications without proper documentation (such as a prescription from a Costa Rican doctor) can lead to suspicion of drug trafficking and legal consequences. It's crucial for visitors to carry a copy of their prescription if bringing medication into the country and be aware of any specific drug regulations before travel.

Penalties

In Costa Rica, drug-related offenses are taken very seriously, and penalties for the possession, trafficking, or use of marijuana, synthetic cannabinoids, and other drugs can be severe. The exact penalty varies depending on the type and amount of drug involved, but the following provides a general overview of the legal consequences:

Marijuana Penalties:

- **Possession of Small Amounts:** For personal use (usually up to 30 grams), the penalty for possession of marijuana can range from **fines** to up to **three years in prison**. However, in practice, Costa Rican authorities may handle small-time offenses with warnings or fines for first-time offenders, though criminal charges are still possible.

- **Trafficking or Distribution:** Trafficking marijuana is a more serious offense. If caught with significant quantities or if found distributing or selling marijuana, penalties can range from **six to 20 years** in prison.

- **Cultivation:** Growing marijuana is also illegal. If authorities find someone cultivating marijuana, they can face penalties similar to those for trafficking, depending on the scale of the cultivation.

Synthetic Cannabinoids Penalties:

- **Possession:** Possessing synthetic cannabinoids is treated similarly to the possession of other illegal drugs. Penalties for possession could range from **fines** to **several years in prison** (up to three years), depending on the amount and the context of the offense.
- **Trafficking:** Trafficking or distribution of synthetic cannabinoids is considered a serious offense, with penalties ranging from **six to 20 years in prison**, depending on the scale of trafficking and the amount involved.

Penalties for Other Drugs:

Cocaine:

- **Possession:** Even small amounts of cocaine can lead to imprisonment, typically ranging from **three to five years** in prison for possession. For larger quantities, the sentence can be much longer.
- **Trafficking:** If caught trafficking cocaine, the penalty is severe, ranging from **eight to 20 years** in prison, depending on the amount and other circumstances of the crime.

Methamphetamines & Heroin:

- **Possession:** Possession of these drugs can lead to penalties ranging from **three years** in prison for small quantities to longer sentences for larger amounts.
- **Trafficking:** Trafficking or distributing methamphetamines or heroin can result in long prison sentences—typically **six to 20 years** or more.

Ecstasy (MDMA), LSD, and Club Drugs:

- **Possession:** Possession of such drugs can lead to **fines** or **imprisonment** for up to **three years** for personal use.

- **Trafficking:** Trafficking in these substances can result in **longer prison sentences**, ranging from **six to 20 years** depending on the quantity and involvement in distribution.

Other Legal Considerations:

- **Trafficking:** If convicted of trafficking any drug, whether it's marijuana, synthetic cannabinoids, or other illicit substances, the penalty can be severe, ranging from six to 20 years in prison, or even longer in extreme cases.
- **Drug Use in Public:** Using drugs in public places (even marijuana or recreational drugs) is **illegal** and could lead to **arrest** or **fines**.
- **Foreign Nationals:** Foreigners caught with drugs in Costa Rica face the same legal consequences as Costa Rican citizens. Additionally, foreign nationals may also face **deportation** if convicted of drug-related crimes.

Prescription Medication

When traveling to Costa Rica with prescription medications, it is essential to ensure that all items are legally permitted. The primary regulation is that travelers must carry their prescription medications in their **original, labeled containers**. Additionally, a **copy of the prescription** or a **letter from the prescribing healthcare provider**, which includes the traveler's name, the medication's generic name, and dosage, is highly recommended. This documentation is crucial if any inquiries arise regarding the medication upon arrival in the country.

Furthermore, travelers should **verify** with the Costa Rican Embassy or relevant authorities to confirm the legal status of their specific medications in Costa Rica. Certain drugs that are common in other nations may be categorized as controlled substances in Costa Rica. It is vital to be aware of these classifications to avoid unintentional violations of local laws.

While over the counter (OTC) medications also fall under regulations, the limitations can vary based on the specific substance. Costa Rica allows travelers to bring **small quantities of OTC** medications for personal use; however, the definition of "small quantities" can differ and is subject to interpretation by law enforcement officials.

OTC medications such as **basic pain relievers, antacids,** and **cold remedies** are generally permitted. However, travelers should be cautious about bringing any medications that have stimulant, sedative, or psychoactive properties, as these may face stricter scrutiny.[10] Similar to prescription medications, it is recommended to carry these drugs in their **original packaging** and to **maintain receipts** or **documentation** demonstrating their legality.

Violating regulations concerning the importation of prescription and over-the-counter medications can lead to severe consequences in Costa Rica. Penalties for possession, use, or trafficking of illegal drugs—including some medications—are strict, with offenders facing hefty fines and imprisonment for serious violations.[11]

Furthermore, travelers should be cognizant of the fact that if their medications fall into the category of controlled substances, they may face particularly harsh penalties, including long jail sentences, depending on the context of their case and the specifics surrounding any perceived trafficking activities.

---

10   https://wwwnc.cdc.gov/travel/destinations/costa-rica/traveler/
     packing-list

11   https://wwwnc.cdc.gov/travel/page/travel-abroad-with-medicine

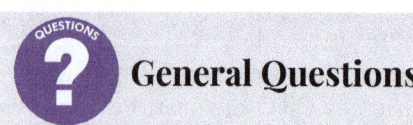

General Questions

1. *Is cannabis legal in Costa Rica?* Cannabis is **illegal for recreational use** in Costa Rica, but **medical cannabis** is legal under strict regulations for certain conditions, with the use of CBD-based products allowed and THC-based products limited to prescribed cases.

2. *Where can I legally purchase marijuana in Costa Rica?* In Costa Rica, you cannot legally purchase marijuana for recreational use, as it remains illegal. However, **medical cannabis** can be obtained through licensed pharmacies or clinics that provide prescriptions for CBD-based products, in compliance with the regulations set by the Ministry of Health.

3. *Can I have marijuana on my person or in my hotel room in Costa Rica?* **No.** You cannot legally have marijuana on your person or in a hotel room in Costa Rica for recreational use, as it remains illegal. Possession of marijuana, even for personal use, can lead to legal consequences, including fines or imprisonment. However, medical cannabis may be allowed if prescribed and obtained through the proper channels, but it must be in compliance with the country's regulations.

4. *Are there any other exceptions to the possession and consumption of cannabis in Costa Rica?* **No.** Besides medical cannabis, there are **no other exceptions** to the possession or consumption of cannabis in Costa Rica. Recreational use remains illegal, and the country does not have provisions for decriminalization or other exceptions outside of medical use. Possessing or consuming cannabis for non-medical purposes can result in legal consequences.

5. ***What are the penalties for possessing and consuming other types of illicit drugs in Costa Rica?*** In Costa Rica, **possession** or **consumption** of illicit drugs such as cocaine, heroin, and methamphetamines can lead to **fines** or up to **3 years in prison**, while trafficking or distribution carries penalties of **6 to 20 years in prison**. The country enforces a strict **zero-tolerance policy** for illegal drugs.

 **Law of the Land Hypothetical**

HYPOTHETICAL: *John, a tourist from the U.S., arrives in Costa Rica and is excited to explore the country. During his stay, he is caught by local police in San José with a small amount of cocaine in his backpack, which he claims was given to him by a friend back home for personal use. He didn't realize that possession of any amount of illicit drugs was illegal, and he now faces legal consequences. What are the potential legal consequences for John, and what can he do to mitigate the situation?*

ANSWER: *John could face severe penalties for possessing cocaine, including a fine or up to 3 years in prison. Costa Rica has a zero-tolerance policy for illegal drugs, and even small amounts are treated seriously. To mitigate the situation, John should contact his embassy immediately for legal assistance and potentially hire a local attorney to help navigate the case. His best defense might be to show a lack of knowledge about Costa Rican drug laws, but possession is still illegal, and the outcome will largely depend on the court's discretion.*

 **Takeaways**

- Costa Rica enforces strict laws regarding the possession and use of both recreational and most medical drugs, including marijuana, synthetic cannabinoids, and other illicit substances. The penalties for possession, trafficking, or distribution can be severe, including imprisonment for up to 20 years.

- While recreational marijuana remains illegal, Costa Rica has legalized medical cannabis for specific conditions under strict regulations, allowing limited use of CBD-based products and heavily restricting THC-based products.

- Synthetic cannabinoids are illegal and carry penalties similar to those for marijuana and other illicit drugs. Costa Rica also has strict laws against the possession and trafficking of hard drugs such as cocaine, methamphetamines, and heroin, with severe consequences for offenders.

- Travelers must carefully follow regulations when bringing prescription medication into Costa Rica, ensuring it is in the original packaging with a valid prescription. Failure to comply with these rules can result in serious legal consequences, including potential imprisonment.

ALCOHOL-RELATED OFFENSES

ALCOHOL-RELATED OFFENSES

Alcohol-Related Offenses

In Costa Rica, **alcohol** has a prominent role in both social and cultural life. Traditionally, alcohol consumption has been woven into everyday activities, especially in social gatherings, festivals, and celebrations. **Beer** is a popular beverage, often consumed with friends and family, and **rum** is another staple drink, reflecting the country's Caribbean influence. Alcohol is also commonly consumed in social events, such as weddings, holidays, or during beach outings.

The country has a **relatively liberal view of alcohol**, with no significant stigma surrounding its use. In fact, Costa Ricans are known for their laid-back attitude toward drinking, often enjoying a drink with meals or at casual social events.

Typical drinks associated with Costa Rica include **Imperial** and **Pilsen**, two of the most popular local beers. Costa Rica is also famous for its **Guaro**, a clear sugarcane liquor often mixed into cocktails or served as shots. Cacique Guaro, in particular, is a well-known brand. Additionally, **fruit-based cocktails**, such as *"fresco de fruta"* (fruit juices with a splash of alcohol), are common in coastal and tourist areas.

Alcohol is legal and widely available in Costa Rica. It can be purchased from supermarkets, convenience stores, bars, restaurants, and tourist shops. The **legal drinking age is 18 years old**, and drinking is generally allowed in public spaces, though there are some local restrictions (e.g., in certain national parks or beaches). **Drunk driving laws** are strictly enforced, with low blood alcohol content (BAC) limits, and offenders face steep fines and potential jail time.

Alcohol Regulation

In Costa Rica, alcohol consumption is governed by several regulations that aim to balance its availability with public safety.

First, **alcohol advertising** is **regulated** to ensure it is not misleading or encouraging excessive drinking. Advertisements are not allowed to target minors or present alcohol in an overly glamorous or excessive light. However, advertising is still prevalent, especially for local beers and Guaro.

Enforcement of alcohol regulations is carried out by local law enforcement, including the *Policía de Tránsito* (traffic police) and municipal authorities. **Drunk driving** is a major focus of enforcement, with strict penalties for those caught exceeding the blood alcohol limit. The legal blood alcohol concentration (BAC) limit for drivers is **0.05%** for private drivers and **0.02%** for commercial drivers. Violators can face heavy fines, license suspension, and even imprisonment in extreme cases.

Regarding **drinking age laws**, the legal drinking age in Costa Rica is **18 years old.** Bars, clubs, and stores selling alcohol are required to verify the age of anyone who appears to be underage. There are also regulations around drinking in public places, particularly in tourist zones, where local authorities may issue fines for public drunkenness or for drinking in restricted areas like national parks.

In general, alcohol regulations are taken seriously in Costa Rica, especially when it comes to public safety, and violations can result in hefty fines or legal consequences.

 **Things to Remember**

- **Drinking Age:** 18 years old

- **ID:** Yes, ID is required to purchase alcohol. Accepted forms include a passport, national ID card, or driver's license.

- **Public Consumption:** Public consumption of alcohol is restricted in some areas, especially near beaches, parks, or national reserves. Local ordinances may vary, but drinking in public spaces like tourist areas or some beaches is typically allowed.

- **Public Drunkenness:** Penalties for public drunkenness include fines or detention for disruptive behavior (e.g., fighting or causing a public disturbance).

- **Drunk Driving:**

  - **Blood Alcohol Limit:** 0.05% for private drivers. 0.02% for commercial drivers.

  - Penalties for exceeding the BAC limit can include fines, license suspension, vehicle impoundment, or even imprisonment in serious cases.

- **Purchase of Alcohol:** Alcohol can be purchased at supermarkets, bars, restaurants, and liquor stores. Restrictions may apply on holidays and Sundays for some sales, especially in rural areas.

- **Alcohol Permits:** If hosting a party or event with alcohol, an alcohol permit may be required, particularly for larger or commercial events. These are typically issued by local authorities or the Ministry of Health.

- **Illegal Alcohol:** The sale of illegal or bootleg alcohol exists but is not widespread. It is regulated by authorities to ensure safety. Unregulated alcohol can pose health risks and is not recommended.

General Questions

6. *Can I drink and drive in Costa Rica?* **No.** You cannot drink and drive in Costa Rica. The legal blood alcohol content (BAC) limit for private drivers is **0.05%**, and for commercial drivers, it is **0.02%**. Penalties for exceeding the BAC limit include fines, license suspension, vehicle impoundment, or even imprisonment, depending on the severity of the offense. It's strongly advised to avoid drinking and driving, as the enforcement of DUI laws is strict.

7. *Can I possess an open container in public?* In Costa Rica, the laws regarding possessing an open container in public vary by location. While drinking alcohol in public is not outright banned, there are **local restrictions** in certain areas, particularly in national parks, beaches, and tourist zones. It's generally allowed in some public spaces, but it's best to check local ordinances, as certain municipalities may impose fines for open containers in specific areas. Always look for signs or inquire locally to avoid penalties.

Law of the Land Hypothetical

HYPOTHETICAL: *Emma, a tourist visiting Costa Rica, is walking down a popular beach promenade in Tamarindo with an open bottle of Imperial beer she bought from a local supermarket. While enjoying her drink and taking in the scenery, she's approached by a local police officer. Can Emma legally drink alcohol in public in Costa Rica, and are there restrictions she should be aware of?*

ANSWER: *In Costa Rica, drinking alcohol in public is generally allowed in many areas, but there are local restrictions, especially in national parks, beaches, and certain tourist zones. In Emma's case, drinking on the beach in Tamarindo may be prohibited due to local ordinances that restrict alcohol consumption in that specific area. While public drinking is not universally banned, Emma should have been aware of these local regulations, as penalties for violating them can include fines. To avoid issues in the future, she should look out for posted signs or inquire with local authorities about any public alcohol restrictions before consuming alcohol in unfamiliar areas.*

 **Takeaways**

- Alcohol, particularly beer and Guaro, plays a central role in Costa Rican culture. It's consumed in social settings, festivals, and gatherings, with no significant stigma surrounding its use. However, there are local regulations regarding public consumption, especially in tourist areas, beaches, and parks.

- Costa Rica has strict drunk driving laws, with a low blood alcohol concentration (BAC) limit of 0.05% for private drivers and 0.02% for commercial drivers. Violators face heavy fines, license suspensions, and potential imprisonment, making it crucial for drivers to avoid drinking and driving.

- While public drinking is generally allowed in some areas, there are local ordinances that restrict open alcohol containers in certain places such as beaches, parks, and national reserves. Tourists should be mindful of these regulations to avoid fines or penalties.

- The legal drinking age in Costa Rica is 18 years old. To purchase alcohol, individuals must present valid ID, such as a passport, national ID, or driver's license. Local authorities enforce this strictly, especially in bars and stores.

FIREARM & AMMUNITION OFFENSES

IN THIS CHAPTER

- Current Firearm Status
- Legal Requirements for Purchasing, Carrying, and Using a Firearm
- Firearm Restrictions for Visitors
- Penalties
- General Questions
- Law of the Land True Story
- Takeaways

CHAPTER 6

FIREARM & AMMUNITION OFFENSES

Current Firearm Status[12]

Costa Rica has developed a comprehensive legal framework governing firearm ownership, reflecting its unique societal contexts and historical background. Following the abolition of its military in 1948, the country established laws aimed at promoting peace and stability while providing specific regulations for firearm ownership and use.

In Costa Rica, only citizens and permanent residents with **a valid residency card** are legally permitted to own, register, and carry firearms. Temporary residents are excluded from owning firearms, highlighting the emphasis placed on stable residency status as a criterion for ownership. This restriction underscores the country's cautious approach to firearm distribution, aiming to ensure that only individuals with long-term commitments to the nation engage in firearm possession.

Costa Rican law classifies firearms into various categories, including **handguns, rifles**, and **shotguns**. According to current legislation, individuals are limited to owning a **maximum of three handguns** and **two long firearms**, contributing to stable and controlled firearm

---

12   https://www.handgunlaw.us/documents/Costa_Rico_Weapons_and_ Explosives_Law_Translation.pdf

ownership. Additionally, Costa Rican law **prohibits** the ownership of **military-grade weapons, automatic firearms**, and **high-caliber rifles**. These limitations reflect the government's focus on public safety and its desire to restrict access to weapons that pose greater dangers.

Legal Requirements for Purchasing, Carrying and Using Firearms

To legally purchase a firearm in Costa Rica, applicants must meet specific criteria stipulated by the Ministry of Public Security and the Department of Arms and Explosives. The requirements for purchasing a firearm include:

- **Eligibility Verification:** Applicants must be citizens or permanent residents. They must provide identification documents, such as their Costa Rican identity card or residency card.

- **Application Submission:** A formal application must be submitted to the Department of Arms and Explosives, detailing the applicant's intent to acquire a firearm, the type of firearm sought, and personal identifiers.

- **Background Checks:** Potential owners must undergo thorough background checks, including the submission of a certificate indicating no criminal record from the Costa Rican judicial authorities.

- **Mental and Physical Fitness Evaluation:** A psychological evaluation conducted by a licensed psychologist is mandatory, ensuring that the potential owner is mentally fit to own and operate a firearm.

- **Training and Examination:** Successful completion of a fire-arms training course and a theoretical-practical examination are prerequisites. This training aims to ensure responsible firearm handling and usage.

Carrying a firearm in public in Costa Rica is subject to strict regulations. An individual must secure a **legal carry permit** in from the Ministry of Public Security in addition to owning a registered firearm. To obtain this permit, a comprehensive application process must be followed, including all the requirements previously mentioned, along with a thorough review by authorities. **Open carry** is **prohibited** in Costa Rica, and firearms should be transported in a locked container when not in use.

The legal carry permits are typically specific to the type of firearm owned. For instance, if an individual receives a permit for a handgun, carrying any other type of firearm without appropriate licensing is illegal. Carrying a firearm without a permit can result in serious penalties, including arrest and prosecution.

The use of firearms is highly regulated in Costa Rica. Firearms should only be used in situations of **legitimate sporting purposes**, **self-defense** or **defense of property**, and **deadly force** can only be employed if there is an imminent threat of harm. Firearms should not be used to settle disputes, and there are severe penalties for the illegal use of a weapon in crimes such as robbery, assault, or threats. Any discharge of a firearm in public or in an unsafe manner can lead to **criminal charges**.

Firearm Restrictions for Visitors[13]

For non-citizens and visitors to Costa Rica, the right to own or carry firearms is virtually nonexistent. While they may temporarily bring sporting firearms into the country for legitimate sporting events (with prior authorization), general ownership or possession rights remain strictly limited to citizens and permanent residents. Visitors must apply for a temporary import permit through the Ministry of Public Security and adhere to the country's import regulations limiting the amount and type of ammunition, as well as the firearms brought into the country.

 For more information on importing firearms to Costa Rica, visit **http://costarica-information.com/about-costa-rica/economy/economic-sectors-industries/real-estate/real-estate-general/moving-to-costa-rica/moving-import/importing-firearms.**

---

13 https://aglegal.com/general/
    costa-rica-gun-laws-what-a-expatriate-need-to-know

If a non-citizen is caught possessing a firearm illegally, they could face severe legal penalties, including **deportation** and **jail time**. Visitors are advised to familiarize themselves with these laws and seek appropriate permits well in advance of travel.

 **Penalties**

Possession of Illegal Firearms

Possessing illegal firearms, such as unregistered weapons, prohibited calibers, or automatic weapons, is a serious offense in Costa Rica. Offenders can face **imprisonment** ranging from **3 to 10 years**, depending on the specific circumstances of the violation, such as the type of firearm and whether the weapon was used in the commission of a crime. In some cases, the court may also impose heavy **fines** on individuals caught with illegal firearms.

Trafficking and Smuggling Firearms

Firearm trafficking and smuggling, whether it involves the importation or exportation of weapons without authorization or their distribution within the country, is severely penalized. Those convicted of firearm trafficking or smuggling can face up to **10 to 15 years** in prison, depending on the scale of the trafficking operation and whether the weapons were intended for criminal organizations. In some cases, criminal fines and asset forfeiture may also apply to those involved in large-scale trafficking or smuggling rings.

Firearm Use in Crimes

The use of firearms in the commission of a crime, such as assault, robbery, or murder, is a grave offense under Costa Rican law. If the firearm is used in the commission of a violent crime, the offender can face increased penalties:

- **For robbery or aggravated assault** involving a firearm, the sentence can be **5 to 10 years** in prison.

- **For murder or attempted murder** using a firearm, the sentence can range from **25 years to life** imprisonment.

- **Additional Circumstances:** If the firearm is used in a **terrorist act** or organized crime, the penalties can be even harsher, and additional charges may be brought, such as terrorism or organized crime involvement.

Unauthorized Carrying of Firearms

Unauthorized carrying of a firearm—whether concealed or not—without the appropriate carry permit is illegal. Individuals caught carrying a firearm without a permit may face:

- **Imprisonment** ranging from **1 to 3 years** for simple offenses.

- If the individual has prior convictions or the firearm is used in the commission of a crime, penalties may be more severe, ranging from **3 to 8 years.**

- If the person carries the firearm in public in a manner deemed dangerous or reckless, additional penalties for **public endangerment** may apply.

Penalties for Organized Crime Involvement

Involvement in organized crime, including trafficking or using firearms for illicit purposes, leads to severe penalties in Costa Rica, particularly for groups engaged in activities like drug trafficking, kidnapping, or extortion. Individuals involved in organized crime related to firearms can face **10 to 20 years** in prison, especially if the crime involves the use of firearms, drugs, or other forms of violence. If the firearms are linked to a **criminal enterprise** or **gang-related activities**, the penalty may be extended to the higher end of the spectrum, and perpetrators may face additional charges under organized crime legislation.

 **General Questions**

8. *What happens if the police catch me carrying a firearm in Costa Rica?* If you're caught carrying a firearm in Costa Rica without proper authorization, the police will seize the weapon, and you may face arrest, fines, and potentially up to 3 years in prison, depending on the circumstances. Additional penalties can apply if the firearm is involved in criminal activity.

9. *What is the potential sentence for a firearms violation upon conviction?* The potential sentence for a firearms violation in Costa Rica can range from a fine to several years in prison, with sentences typically between 2 to 10 years, depending on the severity of the offense (e.g., illegal possession, trafficking, or use in crimes). In some cases, longer sentences may apply if the violation involves organized crime or military-grade weapons.

 **Law of the Land True Story[14]**

Costa Rican authorities have made significant strides in combating illegal firearms in the country, with recent police operations resulting in the confiscation of 757 weapons. These operations, carried out by the

---

14 https://news.co.cr/police-operations-in-costa-rica-manage-to-take-757-firearms-off-of-the-streets/73336/

74

Ministry of Public Security, have primarily targeted individuals without the proper permits to carry firearms. The seized weapons included 338 pistols, 257 revolvers, 45 shotguns, and 40 rifles, among others. The majority of confiscations occurred in San José, Limón, Alajuela, Heredia, and Puntarenas.

Minister of Public Security Michael Soto emphasized the importance of these seizures, noting that firearms are involved in 70% of homicides in Costa Rica. The ongoing efforts, including large-scale "mega-operations," aim to reduce the circulation of illegal weapons and enhance public safety. In addition to firearms, these operations have also resulted in the confiscation of drugs, stolen cattle, and the detention of individuals involved in various criminal activities, including illegal immigration and robbery. The authorities remain committed to strengthening security through continued law enforcement efforts.

 **Takeaways**

- In Costa Rica, only citizens and permanent residents with a valid residency card are allowed to own firearms, with limitations on the number and types of firearms. Military-grade weapons and automatic firearms are strictly prohibited.

- To own a firearm, applicants must undergo background checks, mental fitness evaluations, and firearms training. Carrying a firearm requires a legal permit, and open carry is prohibited.

- Costa Rican law imposes heavy penalties for illegal firearm possession, trafficking, and the use of firearms in crimes, including long prison sentences, particularly for organized crime involvement.

- Non-citizens and visitors in Costa Rica have very limited rights regarding firearms. While they may temporarily import firearms for sporting purposes with prior authorization, they cannot own or carry firearms. Violations can result in severe penalties, including deportation and imprisonment.

CHAPTER 7

PROSTITUTION

IN THIS CHAPTER

- Overview
- Laws and Penalties
- Prostitution Practices
- Sex Trafficking and Exploitation
- Sex Tourism and Public Health
- Tips to Avoid Being Solicited
- Law of the Land Hypothetical
- Takeaways

CHAPTER 7

PROSTITUTION

Overview

Prostitution in Costa Rica is **legal** and **regulated**, distinguishing the country from many of its Central American neighbors. The legal framework operates under a system where sex work itself is not criminalized; however, activities related to prostitution, such as **pimping** and **operating brothels**, are **illegal**. There is a clear distinction between legal prostitution and the illegal exploitation of individuals, with the government working to address human trafficking and sexual exploitation more aggressively in recent years. Despite prostitution being legal, the country still grapples with the consequences of sex tourism and public solicitation, particularly in urban areas or popular tourist spots like **San José**, **Jacó**, and **Limón**.

Several socio-economic factors contribute to the prevalence of prostitution in Costa Rica, particularly **poverty** and **economic inequality**. Many individuals, especially women, may feel that sex work is their only viable option for survival. This is compounded by a lack of accessible job opportunities in certain regions, particularly in rural areas where poverty is more pervasive. For those who migrate to urban centers in search of better prospects, many end up in the sex work industry due to a lack of alternative avenues for employment.

Another key factor driving prostitution in Costa Rica is the booming **sex tourism industry**. The country's tropical climate, beautiful beaches, and relaxed legal environment have long attracted international tourists, some of whom seek out sexual services. The demand for prostitution in tourist-heavy areas like **Jacó** has created an environment where sex work thrives, and, for some, becomes a lucrative business.

In response to these dynamics, Costa Rica has started to shift its approach over the years. Increasingly, there is a focus on **regulations designed to protect sex workers**, such as mandatory health checks for sexually transmitted infections (STIs), including HIV. This regulation aims to reduce public health risks and ensure that those in the industry are safe from the spread of diseases. Additionally, the government has ramped up its efforts to combat **human trafficking** and **sexual exploitation**, particularly of minors. The authorities have worked to crack down on criminal networks involved in trafficking and exploitation, recognizing that many sex workers are coerced or exploited. Local and national law enforcement agencies collaborate to address these concerns through specialized operations that target traffickers and illegal brothels, which are often associated with organized crime.

 ## Laws and Penalties

In Costa Rica, prostitution is primarily governed by **Law No. 7786**, known as the "Law on the Prevention and Control of Sexually Transmitted Infections (STIs), HIV/AIDS, and Other Infectious Diseases". While this law does not explicitly regulate prostitution itself, it has a significant impact on how the sex industry is managed, particularly in terms of public health. This law mandates **regular health check-ups** for sex workers to ensure they are not transmitting sexually transmitted infections (STIs) or HIV/AIDS. These health checks are required to be performed regularly, typically every three months, to ensure the well-being of both sex workers and their clients.

Furthermore, the **Criminal Code of Costa Rica** also includes provisions related to exploitation and trafficking, criminalizing any form of pimping or human trafficking related to prostitution. This ensures that while prostitution is not illegal, any form of coercion, abuse, or involvement of minors is subject to severe legal consequences.

Additionally, **Law No. 7631**, which relates to the **Protection of Minors**, specifically criminalizes any involvement of minors in prostitution, including both sex work and exploitation. The law targets both individuals who engage minors in the trade as well as those who exploit them in any capacity. Additionally, sex workers must be **18 years or older** to participate in the industry legally. If caught violating these age restrictions or engaging in illegal activities, sex workers face significant legal consequences.

Sex workers in Costa Rica must follow a fairly comprehensive process to enter and maintain their profession legally. They must prove their age through a valid ID, submit to health checks, and be verified by local authorities. If a sex worker is caught without the necessary medical proof, they can face fines or be barred from working. The government also mandates that sex workers avoid getting involved in criminal activities, and the penalties for doing so are severe.

Prostitution in Costa Rica is often seen in certain urban areas and tourist-heavy zones, particularly in cities like San José, Jacó, and Limón, where the sex work industry has become somewhat visible. However, Costa Rica doesn't have officially designated zones for prostitution. Instead, it occurs in and around bars, nightclubs, and certain known areas that cater to both locals and visitors. While authorities often overlook street-level sex work in these places, there are no formalized spaces set aside for this purpose.

Though sex work itself is legal, it must be done within the boundaries of the law. Street solicitation, for instance, is prohibited, and anyone caught in the act may face fines or arrest. Furthermore, operating an **unregistered brothel** or offering services outside of the regulatory framework is a punishable offense. The penalties for these infractions vary, but they can include imprisonment or significant fines, depending on the seriousness of the offense.

For **non-citizens** and **visitors**, the situation is clear-cut: they **cannot legally participate in prostitution**. Non-citizens or temporary residents are excluded from owning firearms and cannot engage in sex work, with any involvement leading to serious legal penalties, including deportation or imprisonment.

Prostitution Practices

Prostitution in Costa Rica is widely practiced, though it remains a subject of controversy and complex legal oversight. The country has a largely **tolerant attitude** toward prostitution, as long as it is consensual and does not involve minors or exploitation.

While precise statistics on prostitution in Costa Rica are challenging to obtain, various estimates suggest that there are approximately 15,000 registered sex workers in the country, the majority of which are concentrated in tourist-heavy areas, such as San José, Jacó, and the beaches of Guanacaste. Furthermore, it is estimated that about 80% of the clients engaging in sex tourism come from the United States, reflecting Costa Rica's status as a popular destination for sexual services. A study indicates that up to 10% of tourists visiting Costa Rica engage in sex tourism, highlighting the scale of this phenomenon within the tourism industry.[15]

Prostitution in Costa Rica takes several forms, shaped by socio-economic factors:

- **Street Prostitution:** The most visible form, concentrated in areas like downtown San José, Jacó Beach, and Guanacaste. Street-based workers are vulnerable to abuse and exploitation and typically work near tourist hotspots such as bars, nightclubs, and hotels.
- **Brothels and Escort Services:** While brothels are not explicitly legal, they are often tolerated, especially in tourist areas. These establishments are subject to health regulations. Escort services, which involve pre-arranged meetings, also operate independently but must follow health guidelines.
- **Online Platforms:** With the rise of the internet, online prostitution has grown, allowing workers more control over clients and working hours. However, this comes with legal risks, especially around trafficking concerns.

---

15 https://en.wikipedia.org/wiki/Prostitution_in_Costa_Rica

- **Massage Parlors and Spas:** Some spas and massage parlors discreetly offer sexual services, typically targeting tourists, and operating under the guise of legitimate businesses to avoid legal trouble.

The attitude of local authorities towards prostitution in Costa Rica is complex, balancing regulation, public health, and social stigma. While prostitution is legal, there is significant societal stigma surrounding the industry. Authorities focus on harm reduction and public health, implementing policies such as routine medical exams for registered sex workers to prevent the spread of STIs. However, sex workers often face discrimination and limited access to health services and legal protections. The government also addresses issues like trafficking and exploitation, but its approach tends to be reactive, prioritizing regulatory compliance over tackling the socio-economic factors that drive individuals into sex work.

Sex Trafficking and Exploitation

Sex trafficking and exploitation are significant concerns in Costa Rica, driven by a combination of socio-economic factors, tourism, and organized crime. Despite efforts to combat trafficking, the country remains a source, transit, and destination point for human trafficking, particularly for sex trafficking.

The booming tourism industry plays a significant role in this issue, with foreign visitors flocking to the country for its lively nightlife and more permissive attitudes toward sex. This influx of tourists creates a demand for commercial sex, with certain areas—particularly beach towns like Jacó and Tamarindo, as well as the capital, San José—emerging as hotspots for the exploitation of sex workers, including minors and trafficked individuals.[16]

Vulnerable demographics are especially at risk. **Young women** and **children**, particularly from impoverished or rural backgrounds, are often

---

16 otimes.net/2024/07/31/
    costa-rica-grapples-with-rising-human-trafficking-cases

targeted by traffickers who offer promises of better opportunities, only to coerce them into the sex trade. **Migrants** from neighboring Central American countries, such as Nicaragua, El Salvador, and Honduras, face heightened risks due to their unstable legal status and limited resources. Additionally, **transgender individuals**, who frequently encounter societal discrimination and economic hardship, are also vulnerable to trafficking and forced into sex work.

Combating sex trafficking in Costa Rica faces significant challenges. Weak law enforcement, coupled with corruption within some agencies, hampers efforts to dismantle trafficking networks. Additionally, the high demand for commercial sex, combined with low awareness among tourists and locals about the signs of trafficking, perpetuates the problem. While the government and NGOs have taken steps to address the issue, including legal reforms and awareness campaigns in collaboration with international organizations like the UN, much more needs to be done to tackle the root causes of trafficking and systemic issues that enable it.

 **Sex Tourism and Public Health**

Sex tourism in Costa Rica has become a significant part of the country's tourism industry, driven by its vibrant nightlife, beautiful beaches, and relaxed atmosphere. **Jacó Beach**, on the Pacific Coast, is one of the most famous destinations for sex tourism. With its lively nightlife scene, abundant bars, and nightclubs, Jacó draws a steady flow of both locals and tourists. The beach town is home to street-level prostitution, where foreign visitors seeking quick encounters with sex workers are common.

San José, the bustling capital city, also plays a major role in Costa Rica's sex tourism industry. The city, particularly its red-light districts like Calle de la Amargura, is known for street prostitution. In addition, brothels and escort services cater to tourists seeking paid sex. As the country's transportation hub, San José sees a high influx of international visitors, making it a key location for sex tourism. Similarly, the beach towns of

Guanacaste and **Tamarindo**, located on the Pacific coast, are popular with surfers, vacationers, and sex tourists. The tourism-driven economy here generates demand for both legal and illegal sex work, with many tourists turning to online platforms, brothels, or street-based prostitution to find what they're looking for.

These areas not only cater to the demand for sex but also raise concerns about the ethical implications, public health risks, and exploitation. While Costa Rica continues to attract international visitors, addressing the complexities of sex tourism, including its associated health and social issues, remains an ongoing challenge for the government.

Sex tourism in Costa Rica presents significant public health challenges, particularly the spread of sexually transmitted infections (STIs) like HIV, syphilis, and gonorrhea. While registered sex workers undergo health checks, many unregistered workers, especially those in street-level prostitution, lack access to regular testing and healthcare. Beyond physical health risks, sex workers face mental health issues due to stigma and exploitation, with many suffering from depression, anxiety, and PTSD. Additionally, sex tourism is often linked to human trafficking, particularly involving vulnerable populations like minors and migrants, who may have little access to medical care or psychological support. The lack of comprehensive healthcare and the prevalence of exploitation further complicate these public health concerns.

 ## Tips to Avoid Being Solicited

If you're traveling in Costa Rica and want to avoid being solicited by sex workers, here are some practical tips to help you maintain privacy and avoid unwanted attention:

- **Stay in well-established areas:** Choose reputable hotels or accommodations that are located in safer and more family-oriented areas. Avoid staying in known red-light districts or areas where sex tourism is prevalent, such as downtown San José or Jacó Beach.

- **Be mindful of your surroundings:** Stay alert in high-traffic areas, especially near bars, nightclubs, or areas known for street-level prostitution. If you find yourself in a place where solicitation seems common, consider leaving or heading to a safer location.

- **Dress conservatively:** Dressing modestly, especially in public spaces, can help reduce unwanted attention. Flashy clothing or behavior that could be perceived as an invitation may attract solicitation.

- **Avoid engaging in conversation:** If approached by a sex worker, a simple and polite "no, thank you" or avoiding eye contact can help deter further interaction. It's best to stay firm but non-confrontational.

- **Use direct transportation:** Avoid walking late at night in unfamiliar areas. Opt for taxis or private transportation if you need to get around after dark, especially in neighborhoods known for prostitution.

- **Stay with groups:** If you're traveling with others, stick together, especially when venturing into areas known for nightlife or nightlife-adjacent activities. There's safety in numbers.

 ## Law of the Land Hypothetical

HYPOTHETICAL: *John, a tourist in Jacó Beach, is approached by a young woman offering sex for money. He's unsure if engaging in this transaction could get him in trouble. Is it legal for John to pay for sex, and what are the potential consequences?*

ANSWER: *Prostitution is legal in Costa Rica, but it must occur within regulated environments, such as licensed brothels or with registered sex workers who follow health regulations. Street-level prostitution, often unregulated, carries legal risks. Paying for sex in these contexts could result in fines or legal issues, especially if linked to human trafficking or exploitation. To avoid legal trouble, John should refrain from* *engaging in unregulated sex work and ensure any interactions are with properly licensed services.*

 **Takeaways**

- Prostitution is legal in Costa Rica, but pimping and unregistered brothels are illegal. The government regulates the industry, focusing on health checks and combating human trafficking.

- Poverty and lack of job opportunities, especially in rural areas, drive many into sex work, compounded by the demand from the sex tourism industry in areas like Jacó and San José.

- Sex tourism raises public health risks, particularly the spread of STIs. While registered sex workers undergo health checks, many unregistered workers lack proper healthcare.

- Vulnerable groups, including minors and migrants, are at high risk of trafficking and exploitation, fueled by the demand for sex tourism and weak law enforcement.

CHAPTER 8
LGBTQ

LGBTQ

Homophobia in Costa Rica

Costa Rica has undergone significant shifts in its approach to LGBTQ+ rights, transitioning from a conservative stance influenced by Catholic values to a more progressive outlook. Historically, homosexuality was criminalized, and LGBTQ+ individuals were marginalized, but major changes began in the late 20th century, culminating in the **legalization of same-sex marriage** in **2020**, making Costa Rica the first Central American country to do so.

Cultural attitudes today are generally more accepting, especially in urban areas like San José and Jacó, where younger generations tend to be more supportive of LGBTQ+ rights. However, in **rural areas**, traditional values still hold sway, and **homophobia** can be more pronounced, especially among older generations. The **Catholic Church** continues to influence attitudes, though its power has lessened, and the **machismo culture**, which traditionally enforces rigid gender roles, has contributed to ongoing discrimination.

In Costa Rica, homophobic attitudes, while lessening in recent years, still manifest in various aspects of daily life, particularly in more traditional or rural areas. In the workplace, LGBTQ+ individuals may face subtle or overt discrimination, with many choosing not to openly disclose their sexual orientation for fear of judgment or professional consequences. Schools can be environments where bullying and exclusion occur, especially for students who openly identify as LGBTQ+. In family settings, there are still instances of rejection or resistance, as many parents, influenced by conservative or religious beliefs, may not accept their children's sexuality. While the younger generation in urban centers like San José has become more open-minded, older generations tend to adhere more closely to traditional norms.

Discrimination and **violence against LGBTQ+ people**, unfortunately, continue to be a concern. Reports of hate crimes, verbal abuse, and physical violence persist, though the numbers are difficult to accurately track. According to the Costa Rican LGBTQ+ rights organization, *Acción Diferente*, incidents of violence have been reported, though statistics vary. LGBTQ+ individuals, particularly transgender people, remain at high risk for such violence, with many instances going underreported due to fear of further victimization or police indifference. In the workplace and public life, overt discrimination is illegal, but it still occurs in less visible ways, leaving many members of the LGBTQ+ community vulnerable.

Despite these challenges, there are public figures who have taken strong stances in support of LGBTQ+ rights. Costa Rican activists like Ana de la Reguera and Carlos Alvarado Quesada, the country's former president, have been outspoken advocates for equal rights, including same-sex marriage and anti-discrimination laws. In fact, the government's support for these issues has been pivotal in shifting public opinion over the last decade and Costa Rica is increasingly seen as one of the more progressive countries in Latin America when it comes to LGBTQ+ rights, thanks in part to the advocacy of younger, more secular citizens.

LGBTQ Legislation[17]

Same-sex relationships have been legal in Costa Rica since 1971, when the country decriminalized homosexuality. The penal code has evolved to eliminate previous provisions that punished consensual same-sex relationships, contributing to a legal environment that acknowledges the validity of same-sex partnerships. The influence of both local and international pressures, including human rights advocacy and rulings from

---

17   https://en.wikipedia.org/wiki/LGBTQ_rights_in_Costa_Rica

regional bodies, have spurred legislative changes that promote equality for LGBTQ individuals.

In May **2020, same-sex marriage** was **officially legalized** following a ruling from the Costa Rican Supreme Court that mandated legal recognition of same-sex unions. This landmark decision marked a significant victory for LGBTQ advocates in the country, ensuring that same-sex couples have equal rights under the law, including adoption rights and access to marital benefits. Costa Rica also introduced **anti-discrimination legislation**, which addresses discrimination based on sexual orientation in various aspects of life, including employment and access to goods and services.

Despite this progress, societal attitudes and enforcement of legal protections can be inconsistent, leaving room for discrimination and social ostracism in some contexts. The persistence of conservative elements within Costa Rican society, can challenge the full realization of these rights.

LGBTQ Tourism and Safety Concerns

LGBTQ+ tourism in Costa Rica is **relatively developed**, particularly due to the country's progressive legal framework and reputation as a welcoming and safe destination for LGBTQ+ travelers. Costa Rica's natural beauty, combined with its relatively tolerant attitude toward LGBTQ+ individuals, has made it a popular destination for LGBTQ+ tourists, especially from North America and Europe. The country promotes itself as a destination that embraces diversity, and several businesses cater specifically to LGBTQ+ travelers, offering LGBTQ-friendly accommodations, events, and services.

San José, the capital, is a hub for LGBTQ+ tourism, with a variety of bars, clubs, and cultural events that attract both locals and visitors. The city also hosts the **annual Costa Rica Pride Parade**, a major event in the LGBTQ+ community, which has grown in size and visibility in recent years. In addition, coastal areas like Jacó, Manuel Antonio, and parts of Guanacaste have become well-known for their LGBTQ+ friendly environments, where visitors can find LGBTQ+ welcoming businesses and a more open social atmosphere.

In Costa Rica, **public displays of affection** between LGBTQ+ visitors are generally accepted in urban areas and tourist hotspots, which are known for being more progressive and LGBTQ+ friendly. In these regions, LGBTQ+ tourists can feel relatively comfortable expressing affection in public without significant fear of harassment or discrimination. Major cities also host LGBTQ+ events, further fostering an environment of inclusivity. However, in more rural or conservative areas, PDA between LGBTQ+ individuals might still attract disapproving stares or negative reactions. These areas, influenced by traditional values, may not be as tolerant, and LGBTQ+ visitors may want to be more cautious when it comes to public expressions of affection. While such instances are rare, being mindful of the local cultural context is always recommended in less urbanized areas.

As for **safety concerns**, Costa Rica is considered one of the safer countries in Latin America for LGBTQ+ travelers, particularly in tourist-friendly zones. However, **isolated incidents** of verbal harassment or discrimination can occur, especially in areas where there is less exposure to LGBTQ+ individuals. LGBTQ+ travelers are encouraged to exercise the same level of caution they would in any foreign country, such as avoiding overly secluded areas late at night or being cautious when interacting with strangers. As always when you are traveling, it is important to stay aware of the local cultural and social climate, especially in more conservative areas.

 **General Questions**

1. *Do laws in Costa Rica protect homosexual expressions and conduct?* **Yes.** Costa Rica protects homosexual expressions and conduct. Same-sex sexual activity has been legal since 1971, and in 2020, the country legalized same-sex marriage. LGBTQ+ individuals are also protected by anti-discrimination laws in areas like employment, housing, and access to services.

2. ***What is the punishment for homosexual expressions and conduct?*** There is no punishment for homosexual expressions or conduct in Costa Rica. Homosexuality is legal, and LGBTQ+ individuals are free to express their sexual orientation and engage in same-sex relationships without facing legal penalties, although attitudes in rural areas may be conservative. Costa Rica's legal framework is generally supportive of LGBTQ+ rights, with laws that ensure the protection of individuals' freedoms related to sexuality.

 **Law of the Land True Story**[18]

High-Profile Case. In a landmark event for Costa Rica's LGBTQ+ community, Desiré Stregoni was crowned Miss Gay Costa Rica, a title that will allow her to represent the country at the Central American pageant in El Salvador this November. Stregoni, who works in human resources, used her platform to advocate for LGBTQ+ rights, emphasizing the need for an anti-discrimination law to protect LGBTQ+ individuals, particularly in cases of hate crimes. Costa Rica, while progressive in many areas, lacks specific legal provisions to address hate crimes based on sexual orientation or gender identity.

At the event in San José, which featured various performances, Stregoni's coronation was not only a celebration of drag culture but also a call for greater acceptance and legal protections for marginalized LGBTQ+ groups, particularly trans individuals. The Miss Gay Costa Rica organization highlighted the country's legal advancements, such as civil unions for same-sex couples and the ability for trans individuals to register their names on official documents. However, organizers also acknowledged the persistent challenges posed by conservative attitudes rooted in religion and machismo, which hinder broader societal acceptance of the LGBTQ+ community.

---

18 https://ticotimes.net/2024/09/13/
miss-gay-costa-rica-crowned-championing-lgbtq-rights/

 **Law of the Land Hypothetical**

HYPOTHETICAL: *Ana and Maria, a same-sex couple, have been living together in Costa Rica for several years. They have decided to get married and start a family. While Costa Rica legalized same-sex marriage in 2020, Ana and Maria are unsure about the legal processes involved in changing their legal documents to reflect their new marital status. Can they both change their last names to reflect their married status? And what are the legal steps for adopting a child as a same-sex couple?*

ANSWER: *Ana and Maria are legally allowed to change their last names, as Costa Rica's marriage laws treat same-sex couples the same as heterosexual couples in name change matters. Both spouses can adopt their partner's surname or opt for a hyphenated version, just as in heterosexual marriages.*

Regarding adoption, same-sex couples in Costa Rica have the same legal right to adopt as heterosexual couples since the legalization of same-sex marriage in 2020. The adoption process involves filing with the Costa Rican child welfare agency (PANI) and includes background checks, interviews, and home studies. However, cultural biases or conservative attitudes at some adoption agencies may occasionally cause delays or extra scrutiny, but legally, same-sex couples are entitled to equal adoption rights.

SEXUALLY MOTIVATED/ VIOLENT CRIMES

SEXUALLY MOTIVATED/ VIOLENT CRIMES

Overview

Sexually motivated crimes, including sexual assault and harassment, are a significant issue in Costa Rica, though they are not as prevalent as in some other countries in the region. However, the country faces persistent challenges related to sexual violence, particularly in certain areas. While official statistics are difficult to obtain, reports from local NGOs and law enforcement indicate that sexual violence remains a serious concern.

For example, rare available statistics indicate that the rape rate was approximately 39.4 cases per 100,000 population in 2022, marking a significant public health issue.[19] In 2021, reported rape cases reached 1,786, though it is crucial to note that many incidents go unreported, contributing to an underestimation of the actual prevalence of these crimes. This underreporting is prevalent due to stigma, fear of retaliation, and a lack of faith in the justice system, which further complicates the full understanding of sexual violence in the country.

---

19 https://www.passblue.com/2014/01/08/
    unraveling-sexual-violence-in-costa-rica-and-throughout-latin-america

Contributing factors to the prevalence of sexually motivated crimes in Costa Rica include deep-seated cultural norms surrounding **machismo**, **limited sexual education**, and **economic inequality**. Traditional gender roles, which often emphasize male dominance and female submission, play a major role in shaping attitudes toward women and LGBTQ+ individuals, contributing to the underreporting and normalization of sexual violence. Poverty, unemployment, and lack of opportunities for women, especially in rural areas, also increase vulnerability to exploitation and abuse. Statistics show that domestic violence complaints have surged, with over 30,000 reported cases in the past four years, suggesting an alarming trend fostered by both economic and cultural pressures.[20]

Women, children, and LGBTQ+ individuals are the most affected groups. **Young women**, particularly those from low-income or marginalized communities, are at a higher risk of sexual assault. Statistics reveal that 96% of rape victims are female, with a substantial portion of these victims being adolescents aged between 10 and 19 years old.[21] Moreover, the majority of perpetrators are men, suggesting a stark gender imbalance in the dynamics of these violent acts. **Transgender people** and **sex workers** also face disproportionately high rates of sexual violence and harassment.

There are **regional differences** in the prevalence of sexually motivated crimes, with urban areas like San José and popular tourist destinations like Jacó, Limón, and Guanacaste showing higher rates of sexual violence, often linked to tourism and high levels of sex work. In rural areas, underreporting and cultural taboos make it more difficult to measure the extent of the problem, but vulnerable populations in these regions are often exposed to higher risks due to isolation and lack of resources.

---

20 https://www.passblue.com/2014/01/08/
    unraveling-sexual-violence-in-costa-rica-and-throughout-latin-america

21 https://unsdg.un.org/latest/stories/
    tearing-down-macho-culture-together-costa-rica

Related Legislation

In Costa Rica, sexually motivated crimes are governed by several pieces of legislation that provide legal protection for victims, establish penalties for perpetrators, and guide law enforcement in responding to such crimes. Key legal frameworks addressing sexual violence include:

1. **Criminal Code of Costa Rica:** The Costa Rican Penal Code (Código Penal) criminalizes various forms of sexual violence, including rape, sexual assault, and exploitation.

   - **Rape (Article 152):** Rape is defined as non-consensual sexual intercourse. Penalties for rape can range from **12 to 20 years** in prison, with increased penalties if the victim is a minor, particularly under 15 years old.

   - **Sexual Abuse (Article 156):** Sexual abuse is defined as any sexual act that is not consensual but does not involve penetration. The penalty can range from **4 to 8 years** in prison.

   - **Sexual Exploitation and Trafficking (Article 170):** This section criminalizes sexual exploitation and trafficking, imposing penalties of **up to 20 years** in prison for those involved in the trafficking of minors or adults for sexual purposes.

2. **Law No. 7636 on Domestic Violence:** This law provides additional protections for individuals who are victims of sexual violence within the home, including within intimate partner relationships. It includes provisions that address the prevention, protection, and prosecution of domestic violence, which often overlaps with sexual violence cases.

3. **Law No. 9340 on Sexual Violence:** Costa Rica passed this law in 2016 to strengthen protections for victims of sexual violence, including sexual harassment and exploitation. It includes provisions to improve the legal process for victims, reduce barriers to reporting, and offer additional support for those who come forward. It also expands the definition of sexual violence to include psychological violence and other forms of coercion and abuse, not just physical acts of violence.

4. **Law 9495 on the Protection of Minors:** This law criminalizes the sexual exploitation of minors and increases penalties for offenses committed against children and adolescents. Perpetrators may face **up to 20 years** of imprisonment, especially if the crime involves the abuse or exploitation of children under the age of 15.

5. **Victim Protection Laws:** Costa Rica has provisions to protect victims of sexual violence, especially children and vulnerable adults, including a victim-witness protection program. This includes measures such as anonymous reporting, expedited legal procedures, and support services for victims, particularly those who may fear retaliation or harm from their abusers.

Penalties for sexually motivated crimes vary depending on the severity of the offense. Perpetrators can face long prison sentences, especially for crimes involving minors or aggravated assault. The law also allows for the possibility of parole under certain conditions, but in cases of particularly severe crimes, parole may be denied.

In practice, **enforcement** can be challenging due to underreporting, especially in rural areas or within more conservative communities. Social stigma, lack of education about legal rights, and fear of retaliation can prevent victims from reporting crimes, which makes enforcement more difficult. However, Costa Rica has been working to improve its enforcement capacity by training law enforcement officers, increasing funding for victim support programs, and strengthening the legal process for prosecuting such crimes. The country has also been moving toward a more victim-centered approach to criminal justice in sexual violence cases, prioritizing the protection and rights of victims.

Despite these legislative efforts, challenges remain in ensuring that sexual violence laws are fully enforced, particularly for marginalized groups such as LGBTQ+ individuals, sex workers, and those from lower socio-economic backgrounds.

General Questions

1. ***Do laws in Costa Rica related to sex crimes protect the victims equally?*** **Yes.** Costa Rican laws related to sex crimes are designed to protect all victims equally, regardless of gender, sexual orientation, or other characteristics. The Criminal Code of Costa Rica criminalizes various forms of sexual violence, including rape, sexual assault, and exploitation, with the same penalties applied regardless of the victim's identity.

2. ***Pursuant to law, what is the age of consent for sex in Costa Rica?*** The age of consent for sexual activity in Costa Rica is **15 years old.** According to the Criminal Code (Article 156), sexual relations with individuals under the age of 15 are considered statutory rape and are punishable by law, even if the minor consents. The law also provides enhanced penalties for sexual crimes involving minors, especially in cases where there is coercion or abuse of authority, such as when the perpetrator is an adult in a position of trust (e.g., a teacher or relative).

Law of the Land Hypothetical

HYPOTHETICAL: *Maria, a 25-year-old tourist in Costa Rica, was sexually assaulted while walking back to her hotel. After reporting the crime to the police and undergoing a forensic exam, Maria is concerned about her legal rights as a foreigner. She wonders whether there are special protections for foreigners and if the perpetrator can be prosecuted under Costa Rican law.*

ANSWER: *In Costa Rica, there are no special distinctions made between local and foreign victims of sexually motivated crimes. All individuals, regardless of nationality, are entitled to equal legal protection under Costa Rican law. The perpetrator can be prosecuted for sexual assault* *under local law, and the victim, in this case, Maria, has the same legal rights to pursue justice. Costa Rican authorities are obligated to investigate the crime and ensure that the perpetrator is held accountable, regardless of the victim's nationality.*

Takeaways

- Sexually motivated crimes are a significant issue in Costa Rica, though often underreported due to stigma, fear of retaliation, and mistrust in the justice system.

- Cultural norms like machismo, limited sexual education, and economic inequality contribute to sexual violence, disproportionately affecting women, children, and LGBTQ+ individuals.

- Urban areas like San José and tourist destinations see higher rates of sexual violence, while rural areas face higher risks due to isolation and lack of resources.

- Costa Rica has laws such as the Criminal Code and Law No. 9340 to protect victims and penalize perpetrators, but enforcement is challenging due to cultural attitudes and underreporting, especially among marginalized groups.

ARRESTED IN COSTA RICA

ARRESTED IN COSTA RICA

Overview

When traveling in a foreign country, it's imperative to recognize that you are subject to the legal jurisdiction and regulations of that nation. These laws may significantly differ from those in your home country and might not offer the same legal protections you are accustomed to. It's crucial to bear in mind that penalties for violating foreign laws can be more severe than those for similar offenses in your home country, and ignorance of these laws is not typically accepted as a defense.

The consequences for breaking the law while abroad can be severe and may include expulsion, fines, arrest, or imprisonment. Even unintentional violations can lead to serious legal repercussions. It is essential for travelers to be aware of and adhere to the laws of the host country to avoid legal entanglements and ensure a safe and enjoyable experience.

Specifically, stringent penalties are often enforced for possession, use, or trafficking of illegal drugs in many countries. Convicted offenders can expect severe consequences, including lengthy jail sentences and hefty fines. The legal processes for foreigners in the event of an arrest abroad involve being charged or indicted, prosecuted, potentially convicted and sentenced, and, if applicable, going through an appeals process.

Navigating a foreign legal system can be complex, and individuals arrested abroad must be prepared to comply with the legal procedures of the host country. Seeking legal representation and understanding the local legal nuances are crucial steps for those facing legal issues in a foreign jurisdiction.

Awareness of and adherence to the laws of a foreign country are paramount when traveling. Understanding the potential consequences for legal violations and being prepared to navigate the legal system of the host country are essential aspects of responsible international travel.

Arrest Process[22]

When someone is arrested in Costa Rica, the process begins with the police officer either having a **warrant** or **probable cause** to detain the individual. If they are caught in the act of committing a crime, an arrest can happen immediately. Once detained, the individual is typically taken to a police station for questioning and held for a maximum of **48 hours** before they must be either formally charged or released. During this initial detention period, authorities work with the prosecutor to assess the situation. The prosecutor will decide whether or not to **file charges** against the individual.

If charges are filed, the judicial process proceeds to a **trial** phase, which is usually conducted orally and publicly. Courts in Costa Rica operate without a jury; instead, a single judge or a panel of judges presides over the proceedings, reflecting the Continental European legal tradition. If the judge decides that there's a risk the person might flee or tamper with evidence, the defendant could remain in detention until the trial. Once the legal process continues, a **trial** is scheduled. The accused person has the right to **legal representation**, and if they cannot afford a lawyer, a public defender will be assigned. If convicted, the judge will decide the appropriate **punishment**, which could range from a **fine** or **probation** to **imprisonment**, depending on the crime.

---

22 https://travel.gc.ca/travelling/advisories/
    overview-of-the-criminal-law-system-in-costa-rica

In cases involving **foreigners**, there are some key considerations. Upon arrest, a foreigner has the right to contact their **embassy** or **consulate**. This ensures that they are not deprived of their rights under international law and that **consular assistance** is provided. However, the process can sometimes be more challenging for non-Spanish speakers. If a foreigner does not speak the language, an **interpreter** will be provided during legal proceedings to ensure fair treatment.

Foreigners in Costa Rica are afforded the same **legal rights** and protections as citizens. Yet, some challenges might arise, such as potential misunderstandings about local laws or difficulty navigating the legal system due to language barriers. Furthermore, in serious cases, the individual may face **deportation**, especially if the offense is grave. For example, a convicted foreigner could be expelled from the country after serving a sentence.

Despite these challenges, the Costa Rican legal system ensures that all individuals, regardless of nationality, have access to fair legal processes, including consular assistance and legal representation during their time in custody.

Rights of the Arrested Person

In Costa Rica, the legal framework is designed to ensure that individuals accused of a crime retain **several vital rights** throughout the arrest and detention process. Central to these rights is the Constitution of Costa Rica, which guarantees fundamental protections that are applicable from the moment of arrest. For instance, the Constitution explicitly **prohibits arbitrary detention** and stipulates that an individual cannot be held **without just cause**. This protection underscores the requirement for law enforcement to present a clear rationale for any arrest.

Upon arrest, the detainees must be informed of their rights, including the **right to legal counsel, the cause of their detention,** and **the right** to remain silent.[23] This information is crucial because it ensures that individuals understand their legal status and the nature of the accusations against them. Moreover, individuals have the **right to contact a lawyer** immediately after their arrest. If they cannot afford legal representation, a public defender will be appointed.

Costa Rican law mandates that an arrested person must be presented before a judge **within 24 hours.** This provision helps to prevent prolonged detention without due process and allows an impartial judicial authority to determine the legality of the detention. Furthermore, the law establishes that individuals have the **right to appeal** against their detention and any charges brought against them.

Transparency is also a priority, as criminal proceedings in Costa Rica are typically conducted in an oral and public manner, ensuring that justice is not only carried out but seen to be carried out. This openness prevents possible abuses of power and ensures accountability within the judicial system.

In addition, **foreign citizens** arrested in Costa Rica have the **right to consular notification,** ensuring their embassy is informed of their detention, and the **right to assistance from a lawyer,** including the provision of a public defender if they cannot afford one.

Getting Legal Assistance

If you find yourself arrested while in Costa Rica, the first step is to remain calm and polite. How you respond during the arrest can significantly impact the outcome of the situation. Make sure to inform the arresting officer that you are a foreign citizen and that you wish to contact your country's embassy or consulate. Under international law, you have the right to have your consulate notified of your arrest. This notification is crucial as it can facilitate communication and support from your embassy, which can assist in securing legal representation and providing guidance through the local legal system.

---

23   https://travel.gc.ca/travelling/advisories/
     overview-of-the-criminal-law-system-in-costa-rica

 To report the arrest of a U.S. citizen, you can do so using the U.S. Citizens Services Navigator at **https://cr.usembassy.gov/u-s-citizens-services-navigator/**. The Embassy can help contact family, friends, or employers of the detained U.S. citizen with their written consent, visit the detained U.S. citizen in jail, help ensure that prison officials provide appropriate medical care, explain the local criminal justice and legal processes, and most importantly, connect you to local attorneys who speak English. The local resources are available at **https://cr.usembassy.gov/services/#local**.

Bear in mind, however, that the consular powers are limited, and they cannot get U.S. citizens out of jail, provide legal advice or represent U.S. citizens in court, serve as official interpreters or translators, nor can they pay your legal, medical, or other fees.

Bail

Costa Rica does have a bail system, which is guided by its criminal justice laws. The right to request bail exists for both citizens and foreigners accused of a crime. However, the provision of bail is **highly contingent upon several determining factors**, including the severity of the alleged offense and the individual circumstances of the defendant.[24] Under Costa Rican law judges have considerable discretion in assessing these variables. For more serious crimes, such as those involving violence or significant public threats, bail may be either difficult to obtain or set at prohibitively high amounts, reflecting a broader commitment to protecting public safety within the judicial process.

---

24 https://travel.gc.ca/travelling/advisories/
    overview-of-the-criminal-law-system-in-costa-rica

How Does Bail Work

The bail process in Costa Rica requires the accused to **formally request bail**, which the presiding judge will then consider. The court will evaluate the specifics of the case, including the nature of the crime, existing evidence, and the defendant's history, including any prior criminal records. Bail can take **various forms**, predominantly **financial guarantees** wherein either the defendant or a third party provides a monetary deposit to secure release. Additionally, **non-financial conditions** such as house arrest or travel restrictions may be imposed to ensure compliance with court mandates.

Once bail is granted, the accused must adhere to all stipulated conditions, which are rigorously enforced. **Non-compliance** can lead to **severe penalties**, including the forfeiture of bail and potential re-arrest. This stringent oversight emphasizes the balance the Costa Rican judicial system seeks to maintain—permitting individual liberty while safeguarding public order.[25]

For visitors in Costa Rica, the considerations related to bail are particularly nuanced. **Foreigners** detained for alleged offenses have the same rights to request bail as national citizens. However, it is crucial for visitors to understand that the process may differ in practical terms due to factors such as language barriers or unfamiliarity with local laws. Foreign defendants are strongly advised to seek local legal counsel to navigate the court system effectively and understand the intricacies of their situation.

Moreover, given that the context of the alleged crime can significantly impact bail eligibility, tourists charged with offenses, whether minor or serious, should be mindful that their status as foreigners may influence judicial perceptions regarding flight risk and compliance with court conditions. This underscores the importance of being well-informed about rights and obligations within Costa Rica's legal framework to avoid unintended legal complications while traveling.

---

25 https://bjs.ojp.gov/content/pub/pdf/wfbcjscori.pdf

Complaints Against Police

Costa Rica's police force, historically known for its integrity and neutrality due to the absence of a military, is now facing a crisis of confidence amid rising crime rates and increasing reports of misconduct. While the country has long been seen as peaceful, with no military since 1949 and a commitment to democracy, escalating violence linked to drug trafficking has shaken public trust. In 2023, Costa Rica recorded its highest number of homicides, with around 900 deaths, prompting skepticism about the police's ability to maintain order and safety.[26]

Public opinion polls show a complex relationship with law enforcement. While many citizens express confidence in the police's respect and availability, concerns about police behavior are increasing. Rising crime rates have caused many to question the police's ability to effectively handle organized crime, challenging the force's longstanding reputation for maintaining safety and order. Several common complaints have emerged amid this growing dissatisfaction.

A key issue is the use of **excessive force**, as incidents of police violence have increased alongside rising crime rates, leading to public fear even in the presence of law enforcement. Allegations of police corruption, particularly regarding **bribes** in traffic incidents, further erode trust in the force. Additionally, reports of **police inaction** and reluctance to document crimes contribute to perceptions of inefficiency and a lack of accountability.

Racial profiling is another significant concern, especially among marginalized communities who feel unjustly targeted based on their appearance. Complaints about **insufficient training and professionalism** in the police force also persist, with citizens noting mishandled interactions and inadequate responses to incidents. These issues have fueled protests against police brutality, highlighting public demand for accountability and reform.

---

26 https://cronkitenews.azpbs.org/2024/10/18/
   costa-rica-face-record-breaking-levels-crime-tourists

How to File a Complaint Against the Police

If you find yourself in a situation where you need to file a complaint against the police in Costa Rica, there are several steps you can take to address the issue. The process involves multiple avenues for submitting your concerns, ensuring that you can find a suitable option depending on the nature of the complaint.

To file a criminal complaint against the police in Costa Rica, individuals can submit their "denuncia" to various institutions. Complaints can be filed in person or online, and a complaint form must be completed with detailed information about the incident. It is important to provide supporting evidence like witness statements or photos. After submission, a tracking number is assigned for follow-up, and the complaint will be reviewed to determine if further investigation is needed. While confidentiality can be requested, anonymity may hinder the investigation process.[27]

The first place to turn to is the **Public Prosecutor's Office** (*Ministerio Público*). This office is responsible for investigating criminal acts, including those that may involve police officers. You can file a complaint in person or, if you prefer, use their online portal for convenience. The **Ministerio Público** takes complaints seriously and can launch an investigation into the matter.

 You can get more information about the **Ministerio Público** at **www.ministeriopublico.go.cr** or reach them by phone at **+506 2511-4500**.

Alternatively, if you are concerned about human rights violations or broader issues related to police conduct, the **Ombudsman's Office** (*Defensoría de los Habitantes*) is another key institution that can help. This independent government body is designed to protect the rights of citizens, including any complaints regarding law enforcement.

---

27 https://ticotimes.net/2019/03/22/
    how-to-file-a-criminal-complaint-or-denuncia-in-costa-rica

 You can file a complaint with the **Defensoría de los Habitantes** via their website at **www.defensoria.or.cr**, or by calling **+506 2257-8666**.

If your complaint concerns a specific officer or the professional conduct of the police, the **Professional Responsibility Division of the Ministry of Public Security** (*Ministerio de Seguridad Pública*) may be your next point of contact. This division is tasked with investigating the behavior of individual officers.

 Complaints can be submitted to the **Ministerio de Seguridad Pública** in writing or in person at their office, or you can reach out to them through their website at **www.msp.go.cr** or by calling **+506 2587-2111**.

Additionally, several human rights organizations in Costa Rica can assist with complaints and advocacy. One of these is the *Centro de Estudios para la Democracia* (CED), which works to protect democracy and human rights in the country. They offer support and guidance for those facing human rights violations. You can contact them via their website at **www.cedcr.org**.

Another option is **Amnesty International Costa Rica**, an NGO dedicated to global human rights issues, including police misconduct. Their website is **www.amnistia.cr**, and you can reach them by email at **info@amnistia.cr**.

For more severe cases, you may also consider filing a complaint with the **Inter-American Commission on Human Rights** (CIDH), which is part of the **Organization of American States** (OAS). The CIDH handles human rights complaints across the Americas, including Costa Rica. You can find more information on their website at **https://www.oas.org/es/CIDH**.

General Questions

1. *If I am convicted Costa Rica, am I likely to be released on bail pending the outcome of my appeal?* In Costa Rica, being granted bail after a conviction while awaiting an appeal is possible, but it depends on the nature of the crime. For less serious offenses or if the appeal is based on legal grounds, bail may be allowed. However, for more serious crimes or cases where there's a risk of flight or tampering with evidence, bail is less likely.

2. *What influences a bail determination?* Bail decisions are influenced by factors like the severity of the crime, whether you are considered a flight risk, the potential danger to public safety, and the possibility of reoffending. Your ties to the community, criminal history, and any risk of interfering with the investigation also play a key role in the decision.

3. *Who is entitled to bail?* In Costa Rica, individuals accused of most crimes are **generally entitled to bail**, unless the offense is particularly severe, such as murder or organized crime, or if there are concerns that the person might flee or pose a danger to the public. Bail can be denied in cases where there's a high risk of reoffending or interfering with the investigation. Each case is assessed individually based on the circumstances and the charge.

4. *If I am arrested, how soon will I see a judge or magistrate?* After an arrest in Costa Rica, you must be presented before a judge or magistrate within **48 hours**. This is part of the country's legal requirement to ensure that the detention is lawful and to allow the judge to review the charges against you. If you're not brought before a judge in that time frame, you may be entitled to release.

5. ***Will I be able to contact my country's embassy in Costa Rica?***
Yes. You have the right to contact your country's embassy or consulate in Costa Rica after being arrested. Authorities are generally required to inform you of this right, and you can request to speak with a consular representative. The embassy can offer support, such as legal assistance, and help ensure your rights are respected during the legal process.

JAILS VS. PRISONS: CONDITIONS & CULTURE

JAILS VS. PRISONS: CONDITIONS & CULTURE

Overview[28]

In Costa Rica, the distinction between jails and prisons is clear, but both systems face similar challenges. **Jails** in the country primarily hold individuals awaiting trial or those serving short-term sentences. These facilities are often less secure and are meant for pre-trial detainees or those with sentences of less than three years. **Prisons**, on the other hand, are designed for individuals convicted of more serious crimes, and they house those serving longer sentences. These institutions range from minimum-security facilities to high-security prisons for dangerous offenders.

The Costa Rican penitentiary system is **overseen by the Ministry of Justice and Peace**, which manages both state-run and privately contracted facilities. Despite the efforts to maintain order, **overcrowding** remains one of the system's most pressing issues. Many of the country's jails and prisons are operating beyond capacity, leading to strained resources and diminished conditions for inmates. This overcrowding often results in limited access to healthcare, education, and rehabilitation programs, all of which are essential for reducing recidivism.

---

28 https://crie.cr/what-are-the-jails-like-in-costa-rica/)

Another significant challenge is the **lack of funding**. Prisons in Costa Rica struggle with inadequate financial support, which affects everything from basic living conditions to the availability of staff training and rehabilitation programs. As a result, issues like gang violence and inmate unrest are common, as rival groups vie for control of territories within the facilities, often leading to fights or the spread of illegal activities.

In terms of **rehabilitation**, Costa Rica does offer some programs, but they are not available to all inmates due to resource limitations. Educational programs exist in certain prisons, allowing inmates to earn their high school diplomas or learn vocational skills such as carpentry or welding. These efforts are designed to help with reintegration into society after release. In addition, some prisons provide counseling for mental health and addiction issues, though these services are often limited in scope. Religious programs are another form of support available, with many prisons offering chaplain services and spiritual guidance to inmates.

Despite these programs, the prison system faces a tough road ahead. Overcrowding, lack of funding, and insufficient rehabilitation opportunities mean that many inmates spend their time in conditions that don't help them change or prepare for life after prison. While there are efforts to improve the system, these challenges remain deeply entrenched, making true reform a complex and ongoing process.

Prison Conditions and Living Environment

In Costa Rican prisons, conditions vary based on **security levels**, which range from minimum-security to maximum-security facilities. Minimum-security prisons house individuals convicted of non-violent crimes and offer more freedom, including work and education programs. Maximum-security prisons, for more serious offenders, have stricter controls, with higher surveillance and limited privileges. While this classification aims to reduce violence, overcrowding is a significant issue across all security levels, often leading to cramped and uncomfortable living conditions, even in less-restrictive facilities.

Access to healthcare in Costa Rican prisons is a significant challenge. While inmates are entitled to medical care, the quality and availability are inconsistent due to a shortage of staff and facilities. Basic services, like dental care, are available, but specialized care is scarce. Many prisoners suffer from chronic conditions and mental health issues, but mental health support and addiction treatment programs are limited due to a lack of resources and trained professionals.

Furthermore, **food, sanitation**, and **basic needs** are ongoing concerns. Meals are basic and often lack nutritional balance, with many inmates reporting insufficient food. Family members may provide extra supplies, but this isn't always possible. Sanitation is also a problem, worsened by overcrowding, inadequate bathroom facilities, and poor hygiene standards. Clean water is not always available, and waste disposal is often poor, leading to unsanitary conditions. Basic necessities like clothing, hygiene products, and bedding are often scarce, forcing inmates to rely on family support. These shortages contribute to the discomfort and deprivation many prisoners face.

Inmate Rights and Legal Protections[29]

In Costa Rican prisons, inmate rights and legal protections are guaranteed by the country's constitution and international human rights standards. The Constitution of Costa Rica ensures that all individuals, including prisoners, are **entitled to basic rights** such as **access to justice, humane treatment**, and **protection from cruel or degrading treatment.** Prisoners have the right to be treated with dignity, to not suffer torture or inhumane conditions, and to have access to food, medical care, and legal representation. Additionally, Costa Rica is a signatory to several international human rights conventions, which further protect the rights of prisoners and establish that they must be treated in accordance with international norms.

---

29 https://www.state.gov/reports/2023-coun-
try-reports-on-human-rights-practices/
costa-rica/)

However, despite these constitutional guarantees, challenges persist in the protection of prisoner rights. Access to legal resources and court appeals is limited by overcrowding, lack of access to legal counsel, and the scarcity of educational and legal services within the prison system. Many inmates struggle to file appeals or seek legal recourse due to the limited availability of legal assistance or the difficulty in accessing court systems. Moreover, issues of abuse, both physical and psychological, are reported in some prisons, where overcrowding, lack of supervision, and inadequate staff training can create an environment conducive to mistreatment. Inmates subjected to abuse or violations of their rights often face significant barriers in seeking justice, as the legal recourse mechanisms can be slow, under-resourced, and challenging to navigate without adequate legal representation. While Costa Rican law provides avenues for inmates to file complaints and seek redress, the effectiveness of these measures is often undermined by systemic challenges within the prison system.

General Questions

1. *What is the difference between a jail and prison in Costa Rica?*
   In Costa Rica, jails and prisons serve distinct purposes. Jails are used for short-term detention, typically for individuals awaiting trial or serving sentences under three years. Prisons, however, house those convicted of more serious crimes with longer sentences. Prisons are classified by security levels, from minimum to maximum, depending on the severity of the offenses.

2. *Do jails and prisons offer religious services to inmates?* Yes. Both jails and prisons in Costa Rica typically offer religious services to inmates. Many facilities have chaplains or religious volunteers who provide spiritual support, hold regular religious services, and offer counseling. These services are available to all inmates, regardless of their faith, and are often seen as an important part of rehabilitation and personal reflection during incarceration.

3. ***How do prisoners spend their time?*** In Costa Rican prisons, inmates follow structured routines that include work, meals, and recreation. They can participate in educational programs, vocational training, or religious services. Many work in prison maintenance or labor programs, and some have access to outdoor areas for exercise or group activities, though overcrowding and limited resources can restrict these options.

4. ***What type of jobs can inmates perform?*** In Costa Rican prisons, inmates' time is often structured around daily routines that include work, meals, and recreation. Inmates can participate in educational programs, vocational training, or religious services, depending on the facility. Many spend part of their day working within the prison, either in labor programs or maintaining the facility. For recreation, prisoners may have access to outdoor areas where they can exercise or engage in group activities, though these options can be limited by overcrowding and facility resources.

5. ***How does the prison commissary system work in Costa Rica?*** The prison commissary system in Costa Rica allows inmates to purchase additional items such as snacks, toiletries, and clothing. However, the selection is usually limited, and prices can be high. Inmates typically need to rely on family or friends to deposit money into their accounts, as the government provides minimal personal items. The commissary is often seen as a way for inmates to supplement their basic needs and gain small comforts that are not provided by the prison system.

6. ***What type of medical care do prisoners receive?*** In Costa Rican prisons, inmates receive basic medical care, including general health and dental services, but specialized treatment is limited. Mental health support is scarce, and long wait times for care are common due to overcrowding and resource shortages.

7. *What is prison culture in Costa Rica?* Prison culture in Costa Rica is shaped by overcrowding, limited resources, and inmate alliances for protection. Violence, particularly due to gang rivalries, is common in higher-security facilities. While rehabilitation programs exist, the overall environment is tense, marked by corruption, abuse, and restricted freedoms.

HELPING A FRIEND OR RELATIVE IMPRISONED IN COSTA RICA

HELPING A FRIEND OR RELATIVE IMPRISONED IN COSTA RICA

Overview

If a relative or friend gets arrested in Costa Rica, it's important to act quickly and follow a few key steps.

First, confirm the arrest and location. Contact the Costa Rican police (*Fuerza Pública*) at 800-8000-555 for emergencies, or +506 2527-8000 for general inquiries. Once you know where they're detained, reach out to the Ministry of Justice (*Ministerio de Justicia y Paz*) for further details. Understanding the legal process is crucial so your next step should be to contact a local lawyer who knows Costa Rican law and can assist with bail, legal representation, and navigating the legal process. Contact your home embassy for lawyer recommendations, or search online for reputable legal resources.

 The U.S. embassy maintains a list of local English-speaking attorneys, which can be accessed at **https://common.usembassy.gov/wp-content/uploads/sites/129/2024/01/list-attorneys.pdf**

You should maintain contact with your country's embassy or consulate as they can ensure fair treatment, provide a list of local lawyers, assist with communication if needed, and help arrange money transfers for legal or personal expenses. You may also need to send money for things like food, hygiene, or phone calls. The embassy can help you with this process.

It's important to stay in touch with your loved one. Costa Rican prisons allow visitation, but rules vary by facility. You can contact the detention center to confirm visitation hours, letter sending rules, and phone call permissions. If visiting isn't possible, embassy staff can arrange consular visits. If you believe your loved one is being mistreated, contact the *Defensoría de los Habitantes* (Ombudsman) or your embassy. They can investigate complaints about mistreatment and ensure international human rights standards are upheld.

By staying organized, seeking legal support, and working with your embassy, you can help your loved one through this process and ensure their rights are protected.

Sending Food, Supplies, and Money to an Inmate

In most Costa Rican prisons, family and friends are **not allowed to bring food directly to inmates** unless there are specific permissions granted by the facility. The general rule is that prisoners typically receive food through the prison system, but the quality may be basic, and inmates sometimes need additional supplies.

If the facility does allow outside food, the types of food allowed often depend on security and hygiene considerations. Typically, food must be **prepackaged** and **sealed**, and some prisons may not allow homemade food. Each prison may have different rules, but **perishable foods** like fresh fruits, vegetables, or meats are usually **not allowed. Canned goods** are often more acceptable, as long as they are factory sealed. To find out the exact rules for sending food, you should contact the specific facility where the inmate is being held.

Prisons in Costa Rica generally allow inmates to receive **packages**, but these too are subject to **strict rules.**

- **Approved items:** Common items that can typically be sent include hygiene products (soap, toothpaste), clothing (underwear, socks), and small personal items (books, magazines, religious materials).
- **Prohibited items:** Generally, drugs, alcohol, sharp objects, weapons, and anything that could pose a security risk are strictly forbidden. Electronics, such as phones or music players, are also not allowed.

Each facility has its own regulations about the types of items that can be sent, so it's essential to confirm directly with the prison or jail where the inmate is located. Some facilities may require that packages be sent through a specific delivery service, or you may need to drop them off in person.

Mail, Phone Calls, and Visitation

Phone Calls

In Costa Rica, inmates are **not allowed to have personal cell phones** in prison. Security regulations prohibit prisoners from possessing mobile phones, as they could be used for illegal activities. However, some prisons may allow inmates to make calls under supervision.

Inmates in Costa Rican prisons generally **can make and receive calls**, but the process is controlled. They typically need to make calls through prison-operated phone systems. This system may require the inmate to have money in their commissary account to cover the cost of calls. Calls are often **monitored** for security purposes and may be limited in duration.

- **Outgoing calls:** Inmates can usually make calls, but they may only be allowed to call certain numbers that have been pre-approved by the prison. Calls are generally collect, and the recipient (you) is responsible for paying the charges.

- **Incoming calls:** Most prisons do **not allow incoming calls.** Family members or friends cannot directly call an inmate. Instead, the inmate must initiate the call.

Policies on phone access can vary slightly depending on the prison, but there are some general guidelines. Phone access is typically **limited to specific hours** and may be restricted to weekends or designated days. Inmates may be required to request phone time in advance, and they usually can only call people who are on an approved list. The duration of calls can also be restricted.

Visitation

Visiting an incarcerated family member or friend in Costa Rica requires following specific rules, which can vary by prison. Generally, **immediate family members** (parents, siblings, spouses, and children) are allowed to visit, and **close friends** may be permitted with prior approval. **Lawyers** and **embassy staff** also have special visitation rights. Inmates typically receive **one or two visits per week**, but this can depend on the facility. It's important to **check visiting hours** and schedule in advance, especially in high-security prisons.

Upon arrival, visitors must present a valid **photo ID** and may need to be **approved in advance.** Expect a **security check** that includes passing through metal detectors and having your belongings searched. Once inside, visits are often held through a glass partition, with **limited physical contact.** In some places, brief handshakes may be permitted, but hugs or kisses are usually not.

Dress codes typically require closed-toe shoes and appropriate attire (no revealing clothing). Visits are usually **time-limited** (about 30 minutes to 1 hour), so arriving on time is essential. Be aware that **visits are monitored** for security.[30]

---

30 https://www.allworld.com/costa-rica-prisons/

Prison Scams

When a loved one is incarcerated in Costa Rica, the emotional toll can be overwhelming, and unfortunately, scammers often prey on families in this vulnerable situation. These fraudsters know that families are under stress and may act impulsively when they receive unexpected, urgent messages. Whether it's a phone call claiming the inmate is in danger or a fraudulent request for bail money, these scams can be both emotionally and financially devastating.

One common scam involves someone pretending to be a **prison official** or a **lawyer**. They'll tell you that your loved one needs immediate financial assistance—whether it's for a medical emergency, to pay a bribe, or to secure an early release. They might demand a large sum of money, often with a sense of **urgency**, pressuring you to act fast. The scammer may be convincing, using official-sounding titles or even an inmate's name, but once the money is sent, you'll quickly realize it's gone with no way to recover it.

Another scam is the **fake collect call**, where a scammer tricks the prison's phone system to make it seem like it's coming from your loved one. The caller might claim they're in trouble and need money to get out of a dangerous situation or to settle some kind of issue. They'll ask for money, credit card information, or personal details, always emphasizing the urgency of the situation. It's a highly effective tactic because it preys on your natural desire to help your family member in crisis. Then, there are **false donation requests**, where someone pretends to represent a charitable organization collecting money for the prison. They may claim they're raising funds for educational programs, medical needs, or better living conditions for inmates. The requests may seem noble or even tax-deductible, but they're just another way for criminals to line their pockets.

To protect yourself from falling victim you first have to recognize the **red flags**. Scammers often create a sense of urgency—they want you to make a decision quickly without taking the time to think it through. If someone is pressuring you for money, especially if they want it via untraceable means like wire transfers or prepaid gift cards, it's a major red flag. Official procedures, especially in legal matters like bail, are rarely as fast or as simple as scammers make them seem.

If you suspect something is wrong, **stop communication immediately**. Don't respond to emails, calls, or texts. Instead, **verify the situation** by contacting the prison directly. Call the facility where your loved one is held to check if they're in any kind of trouble or if the request is legitimate. Always use official contact information—never trust the details a scammer provides. If they claim to be a lawyer, consult a lawyer you trust to confirm whether the request makes sense.

If you've already been scammed, **document everything**—save all messages, call records, and receipts—and report the incident to the local authorities. In Costa Rica, you can contact the Fuerza Pública (National Police) or the OIJ (Organismo de Investigación Judicial), which handles fraud cases. If you're a foreign national, it's also wise to reach out to your embassy or consulate for assistance. They can guide you through the reporting process and help protect your interests.

Finally, educate yourself and others. Make sure family members or friends who might also be in contact with the inmate are aware of these scams. The more people are informed, the less likely they are to fall for these manipulative tactics.

Upon Release

When a foreigner is released from prison in Costa Rica, the process can be complex, with several legal and immigration considerations. After their release, the individual may face **deportation** if they were convicted of a serious crime, particularly drug offenses. Immigration authorities typically step in, checking their legal status and potentially issuing a **deportation order**, which may include a **ban on re-entering** the country for a specific time or indefinitely.

Beyond immigration issues, a released foreigner may still be subject to legal obligations like **probation** or **parole**, which include regular check-ins with a probation officer. If they're under probation, they may also face **restrictions on travel** and need permission before leaving the country. Some individuals are required to **pay restitution** or fines, and there could be **restraining orders** preventing contact with victims or specific locations.

Foreigners may also need to work with their embassy for exit visas or other travel documentation, especially if deportation is involved. They may face practical difficulties in finding housing or employment and may need assistance in returning to their home country.

In short, while the release of a foreign national from Costa Rican prison provides some relief, there are significant legal and immigration challenges ahead, including the possibility of deportation, probation, and travel restrictions. It's crucial for the individual to understand and follow any legal requirements to avoid further complications.

THE ADMINISTRATION OF JUSTICE

THE ADMINISTRATION OF JUSTICE

Costa Rica's Legal System

Costa Rica's legal system is deeply rooted in its colonial past and its commitment to democratic principles. Originally shaped by Spanish colonial law, the country's legal framework was influenced by Roman law, particularly the Napoleonic Code, which continues to play a central role today. After Costa Rica gained independence from Spain in 1821 and later formed its own republic, it began establishing a legal structure grounded in constitutional law. The **Constitution of 1859** laid the foundation for the modern legal system, guaranteeing democratic governance and individual rights, and it has been amended over time to ensure the protection of human rights and adapt to evolving legal standards.

Costa Rica's **Constitution**, which is the highest law in the land, divides powers between the executive, legislative, and judicial branches of government, each with distinct responsibilities. The **judiciary** is an independent body responsible for interpreting the laws and the Constitution. The **Supreme Court**, the highest judicial authority, has the final say on legal matters, and the lower courts handle criminal, civil, and administrative cases. Costa Rica operates under a **civil law system**, where written codes—such as the Civil Code and Criminal Code—form the basis of legal practice. These codes govern aspects like personal rights, contracts, property, and criminal behavior.

Another key institution in the Costa Rican legal landscape is the **Public Ministry** (*Ministerio Público*), an independent body tasked with prosecuting criminal cases on behalf of the state. Prosecutors in this office ensure that justice is carried out, investigating crimes and bringing them to trial. The **executive branch,** led by the President, oversees the enforcement of laws and executive orders, while the **legislature,** a unicameral body, creates new laws and amendments. The Costa Rican *Asamblea Legislativa* is responsible for passing new statutes and reviewing existing ones, ensuring that the legal framework adapts to the needs of society.

Costa Rica's legal system is also marked by its strong commitment to human rights. The country is a leader in the international **human rights** movement, playing an active role in the Inter-American Court of Human Rights. The Constitution guarantees the protection of fundamental rights and freedoms, which the judiciary enforces. Furthermore, Costa Rica incorporates **international law** into its legal framework, participating in various treaties and conventions on human rights, trade, and environmental protection.

The country's legal system places a significant emphasis on **environmental law,** reflecting Costa Rica's global reputation as a leader in conservation. The legal framework includes stringent protections for the country's biodiversity, national parks, and protected areas, ensuring sustainable land use and conservation efforts.

However, the judiciary faces **several challenges.** One significant issue is **backlogs in the court system,** leading to delays in resolving cases, especially in civil and family courts. This congestion affects the timely delivery of justice. Another challenge is the **perception of corruption** in some sectors of the judiciary, which, although generally well-regarded, has been the subject of occasional scandals. Lastly, there is a need for **greater access to justice** for marginalized communities, particularly in rural areas, where legal services can be limited. Despite these challenges, Costa Rica remains one of the most stable and respected judicial systems in the region.

General Questions

1. *Will the court treat first-time offenders and tourists with more leniency?* In Costa Rica, first-time offenders and tourists may receive some leniency, particularly for minor offenses like petty theft or low-level drug possession. Alternatives such as fines or community service are possible for less serious crimes. However, for more severe offenses like drug trafficking or violent crimes, leniency is less likely, and the law is generally applied consistently regardless of the person's background.

2. *If I am charged with a crime, which court is likely to hear my case?* If you are charged with a crime in Costa Rica, the case will likely be heard in a criminal court, depending on the severity of the charge. Minor offenses may be handled by local courts, while serious crimes are processed by higher courts, such as trial courts in the district where the crime occurred. For appeals or more complex cases, the Court of Appeals may review the matter. In certain situations, if an individual is facing immigration-related charges or issues tied to foreign status, their case might be handled with the involvement of immigration authorities or specific legal tribunals.

3. *What is the standard of proof in a criminal case in Costa Rica?* The standard of proof in Costa Rican criminal cases is **"beyond a reasonable doubt"**, similar to many other civil law systems. This means that the prosecution must provide sufficient evidence to convince the judge(s) of the defendant's guilt to the point where no reasonable doubt remains. This is a high burden of proof, and the defense has the right to challenge the evidence and present their own. If the prosecution fails to meet this standard, the defendant will be acquitted. Costa Rica's trial system generally emphasizes the collection of evidence and facts, requiring clear documentation and testimony to support the charges.

Law of the Land True Story

At the end of 2024, Costa Rica strengthened its commitment to restorative justice with the introduction of a new protocol aimed at providing alternatives to incarceration for women in vulnerable situations who commit minor drug offenses. Developed by the Judicial Branch in collaboration with the Costa Rican Institute on Drugs (ICD) and the Institute on Alcoholism and Drug Dependency (IAFA), with technical support from the European Union's COPOLAD III Program, the protocol focuses on rehabilitation and social reintegration rather than punishment.

The protocol adopts a restorative, gender-sensitive approach focused on reducing recidivism and supporting the reintegration of women offenders into society. Aligning with international human rights standards, it positions Costa Rica as a regional leader in humane, inclusive criminal justice. European Union Ambassador Pierre-Louis Lempereur praised its focus on reparation and inclusion, addressing structural inequalities, and ensuring gender-sensitive justice. The initiative involves coordination among multiple institutions, including the EU Delegation, the Ministry of Justice, and social organizations. Part of a regional COPOLAD effort, it aims to serve as a model for other Latin American and Caribbean countries, promoting restorative justice and human rights.

Takeaways

- Costa Rica's legal system is based on Roman law and the Napoleonic Code, shaped by its colonial past and the 1859 Constitution, which ensures democratic governance, individual rights, and a balanced separation of powers among the executive, legislative, and judicial branches.

- Costa Rica is a leader in human rights, actively participating in international human rights bodies like the Inter-American Court of Human Rights. It also emphasizes environmental law, with strong protections for its biodiversity and natural resources.

- Despite its stable legal system, Costa Rica faces challenges such as court backlogs, occasional corruption scandals, and limited access to justice for marginalized communities, particularly in rural areas.

CHAPTER 14
CRIME VICTIM ASSISTANCE

CHAPTER 14

CRIME VICTIM ASSISTANCE

Overview

Costa Rica offers a range of resources for crime victims, which include legal, medical, and psychological support. The **Office for the Attention and Protection of the Victim** (OAPVD) is a key entity responsible for assisting victims, providing psychological care, legal advice, and connections to social support networks. They also provide individual and group sessions to help victims cope with the emotional impact of criminal incidents.[31]

Moreover, victims are encouraged to report crimes to the **Judicial Investigation Agency** (OIJ), which plays a crucial role in the law enforcement system. This agency works closely with victims to collect evidence and ensure that legal proceedings are initiated. Victims can also receive medical assistance through local healthcare facilities, which offer services related to injuries sustained during criminal events.

Additionally, the **Ministry of Justice and Peace** manages programs to assist victims, especially in cases of domestic violence, sexual assault, and human trafficking, while the **National Institute for Women** (INAMU)

---

31 https://ministeriopublico.poder-judicial.go.cr/images/Documentos/
   OAPVD/ot.-54645-folleto-oficina-de-atencion-y-proteccion-version-en-
   ingles.pdf

also offers support to female victims of gender-based violence, providing shelters, legal aid, and counseling services.

Various non-governmental organizations (NGOs) also play a crucial role in supporting crime victims. **Red de Mujeres** (Women's Network) offers specialized services for female victims of violence, including counseling, legal advice, and emergency shelter. Other organizations, like **Casa de la Mujer** and **Fundación Mujer y Familia,** provide resources and protection for victims of domestic violence and sexual abuse. **Fundación Paniamor** works with children and families, providing support for minors who have suffered abuse or neglect.

For immediate help, victims can contact emergency services through the following numbers:

- **Police:** 911 (emergency number for police, fire, and ambulance)
- **Domestic Violence:** 800-00-165-16 (INAMU's hotline for assistance in cases of gender-based violence)
- **Victim Assistance:** 800-800-8090 (Victim Support Office hotline)

These resources aim to provide immediate assistance, as well as long-term support to help victims of crime recover and seek justice.

What to Do If You Are the Victim of a Crime

If you're a foreign visitor to Costa Rica and become a crime victim, there are several steps you should take to ensure your safety and get the help you need.

First, you should report the crime immediately by calling **911** or heading to the nearest police station. It's important to get a **police report**, as this will be needed for insurance claims or any legal actions. If you're not fluent in Spanish, it can be useful to have a **translator** with you, especially when dealing with authorities or medical services.

Your **embassy or consulate** can be a key resource. They can't directly intervene in legal matters, but they can assist you with **replacing lost passports**, connecting you with **legal help**, or referring you to **local victim support organizations**. They can also offer general guidance throughout the process.

Language barriers can be a challenge, so it's helpful to know that some victim support organizations offer **bilingual services**. These include **NGOs** like Red de Mujeres and Paniamor, which provide legal advice and psychological support to victims of crime. Many of these groups also help navigate the local legal system.

If you have **travel or health insurance**, be sure to reach out to your provider for any medical expenses or property losses related to the crime. While Costa Rica doesn't have a national victim compensation program, you may still be able to seek **compensation** if the perpetrator is caught.

Lastly, **stay cautious**, especially in tourist-heavy areas, where theft and scams are more common. If you're staying in Costa Rica for an extended period during legal proceedings, your embassy can assist with staying in touch with authorities and providing ongoing support.

Common Tourist Scams in Costa Rica[32]

When visiting Costa Rica, it's important to be aware of common scams that target tourists. While the country is generally safe, knowing what to look out for can help you avoid pitfalls.

One common scam involves **taxis**. Unofficial taxis at airports or tourist spots may offer rides at inflated prices, sometimes claiming the meter is broken. Always use official red taxis with a meter or agree on the fare in advance.

Fake tours are also common. Street vendors or individuals may promise discounted or exclusive activities, but these often turn out to be subpar

---

32 https://mytanfeet.com/costa-rica-travel-tips/costa-rica-tourist-scams/

or non-existent. To avoid this, book tours through reputable companies after researching in advance.

Pickpocketing occurs in crowded areas like markets and bus stations, where thieves often work in pairs. Keep valuables in a money belt or front pockets and stay alert to distractions.

Some scammers offer **"free" gifts** or services, like flowers or photos, and demand payment once accepted. If something seems too good to be true, politely decline.

Another risk is **ATM skimming**. Stick to ATMs in bank branches or shopping malls and check for any unusual attachments before using them.

Timeshare schemes are also common, where tourists are lured by "free" gifts in exchange for attending high-pressure sales pitches. Be cautious with unsolicited timeshare offers.

In tourist areas, **overpriced souvenirs or services** can be a problem. Always ask for the price upfront, shop around, and avoid being pressured into buying something unnecessary.

Lastly, beware of **police impersonators** who may ask for bribes. Always ask to see a badge or ID and call the local police if you're unsure. To protect yourself, stay informed, trust your instincts, and use reputable services. Secure your belongings, and if you encounter a scam, report it to the local tourist police or your embassy.

Sexual Assault

If you're a victim of sexual assault in Costa Rica, your first priority is to ensure your safety. Immediately remove yourself from the situation and get to a safe location. **Call emergency services at 911** to report the assault or seek immediate help. You can also contact the **tourist police**, who are trained to assist foreign nationals ((506) 2258-1008 or (506)

2258-1022; policia_turistica@msp.go.cr). If you are unable to call, seek help from a nearby business or passersby.

Once you are safe, it's essential to **report the incident**. Sexual assault should be reported to local authorities. You can file a report at a police station, and there are special units dedicated to handling cases involving tourists. The police will guide you through the process and explain your options for pursuing legal action. **Seek medical attention** right away to receive care and preserve evidence, as this may be critical in a legal case. Hospitals and clinics in Costa Rica are equipped to provide treatment and support in sexual assault cases.

As a victim of sexual assault, you have the **right to privacy**, medical care, and emotional support throughout the legal process. Costa Rican law offers protections for victims, including access to counseling and legal aid. NGOs, such as INAMU (National Institute for Women), can provide further assistance and help navigate the legal and emotional challenges of the situation.

For your safety while traveling, it's important to take precautions such as avoiding isolated areas, especially at night, and staying in well-populated, well-lit areas. Travel with trusted companions when possible and remain vigilant in unfamiliar environments. If an assault does occur, act swiftly to ensure your safety, report the incident, and know that there are resources and legal protections available to help you through the process.

Consular Assistance

If you find yourself in need of help while in Costa Rica, your **embassy or consulate** can be an **essential resource**, especially in cases involving legal issues, lost passports, medical emergencies, or victimization. Embassies offer a variety of services to citizens, including **emergency travel documents**, **legal assistance referrals**, and **contacting family members** in case of an emergency. If you're a victim of crime or an accident, the embassy can help you connect with local authorities and provide information on how to navigate the local legal system.

Consular assistance can also extend to providing lists of local doctors, lawyers, and translators, and assisting with arranging **medical evacuations** if needed. Additionally, they can assist in cases of **arrests**, offering guidance on your rights and helping ensure that you're treated fairly under Costa Rican law. In cases of serious injury or death, the consulate can provide support with **repatriation of remains** or contacting family members back home.

However, it's important to understand that there are **limitations** to consular assistance. Embassies cannot intervene in legal matters or alter the outcome of a court case. They also cannot pay fines, legal fees, or offer financial assistance, except in limited emergency situations. Furthermore, they cannot represent you in court, negotiate with local authorities on your behalf, or get you out of jail if you are arrested. Their role is to ensure your safety, provide information, and offer support, but they must respect the local legal framework and cannot overstep their jurisdiction.

 ## General Questions

1. *If I am a victim of a crime, can I legally be compensated?*
   Yes. In Costa Rica, victims of certain crimes, including violent crimes, may be eligible for compensation. This compensation typically covers medical expenses, lost wages, and other damages. However, this process can be complex and may require legal assistance to navigate. It's also worth noting that the amount of compensation may be limited and not guaranteed for every crime.

2. ***If a family member falls victim to homicide, can I bring the body back to my home country?*** **Yes.** If a family member falls victim to homicide in Costa Rica, you can repatriate the body to your home country. The process involves coordination between local authorities, funeral homes, and your embassy or consulate. They can assist with legal requirements, documentation, and transportation. The family will need to cover the costs of repatriation, and it may take some time due to legal and bureaucratic procedures.

3. ***If a family member falls victim to homicide, will I receive any assistance from the Costa Rican government?*** While Costa Rica does not have a specific program offering direct financial assistance to families of homicide victims, the Costa Rican government can provide support through law enforcement, including helping with the investigation. The Public Ministry may keep the family informed of legal proceedings, and the embassy can assist with coordinating resources and legal advice, especially for foreign nationals. The Ministry of Health can offer psychological support, but families should also seek additional counseling or legal help if needed.

Safety Tips

- Take official red taxis with meters and book tours through reputable companies.

- Carry minimal cash and use a money belt. Keep valuables in a hotel safe.

- Avoid "free" gifts or offers, timeshare schemes, and check for ATM skimming devices.

- Always ask to see ID if approached by someone claiming to be a police officer. Call authorities if unsure.

- Don't share personal info with strangers, stay in well-lit areas, and trust your instincts.

- Keep emergency contacts handy (e.g., 911 for police) and stay informed on local laws.

POLICE

POLICE

Overview[33]

Costa Rica's police force is structured into several key units, each with distinct responsibilities, but they operate under the oversight of the **Ministry of Public Security**. The primary law enforcement agencies are:

- **Public Force (Fuerza Pública):** The main national police force, responsible for maintaining public order, enforcing laws, and ensuring the safety of citizens. They handle criminal investigations, crowd control, and general law enforcement duties. They are stationed throughout the country and are the most visible police presence.

- **Traffic Police (Policía de Tránsito):** A specialized unit that manages traffic laws, road safety, and accidents. They monitor highways and urban traffic, enforce traffic regulations, and investigate related offenses.

- **Tourist Police (Policía Turistíca):** Focused on ensuring the safety of foreign visitors, they are stationed in tourist areas and handle crimes involving tourists, providing a link between visitors and the broader justice system.

- **Municipal Police:** Local police forces that operate in specific municipalities, often focusing on local ordinances, urban policing, and

---

33 https://costarica.fandom.com/wiki/Police_forces

minor offenses like noise complaints and zoning violations. Their jurisdiction is limited to the municipality they serve.

In terms of size, Costa Rica's police force is estimated to be around 14,500 officers to serve a population of around 5 million residents.[34] This equates to roughly 290 police officers per 100,000 inhabitants, which is relatively low compared to global standards. For instance, the United Nations reports a median ratio of 300 police officers per 100,000 inhabitants, suggesting that Costa Rica's police force is marginally under this benchmark. While adequate for basic law enforcement, there have been concerns about **staffing shortages**, especially in rural areas, which can lead to delays in response times and challenges in effectively combating crime.

Though Costa Rica has a relatively low crime rate compared to other countries in the region, the police force faces increasing challenges with organized crime, drug trafficking, and property crimes, leading to calls for increased funding, better training, and more personnel to maintain security. Some areas of the police force are considered **understaffed**, especially given the country's growing population and tourism industry, requiring ongoing reform and investment to ensure an effective response to modern security concerns.

Police Response

The police force in Costa Rica, particularly the Fuerza Pública, plays a crucial role in maintaining public order and safety. Its **key functions** include general patrol, crime prevention, and the enforcement of laws against various offenses such as drug trafficking, theft, and violence. Officers are responsible for responding to emergencies, managing public events, and safeguarding both local communities and tourists. Additionally, specialized units, like the Judicial Investigation Police (OIJ), are charged with ensuring thorough investigations into serious

---

34 https://en.wikipedia.org/wiki/
List_of_countries_and_dependencies_by_number_of_police_officers

crimes, which adds a critical dimension to law enforcement capabilities in the country (Costa Rica - Interpol).

Challenges facing Costa Rica's police force include increasing crime rates, particularly **drug-related violence** and **organized crime**, which have grown due to the country's location as a drug transit route. Additionally, there are concerns about **corruption** within some sectors of the police and challenges related to **understaffing** in rural areas, which affects response times and policing effectiveness. There is also a growing concern about **police relations with marginalized communities**, where lack of trust may hinder effective law enforcement.

Costa Rica has been implementing **important reforms** to address these challenges. One major initiative is the modernization of police training, focusing on human rights, transparency, and community-based policing. The government has also emphasized improving the use of technology in law enforcement, enhancing surveillance systems, and integrating databases to combat crime more efficiently. Additionally, there are ongoing efforts to improve inter-institutional coordination, with a focus on better cooperation between the police, the judiciary, and social organizations to address crime more comprehensively. Despite these reforms, funding shortages and the complexity of organized crime remain significant hurdles.

Police and Community Relations

The overall image and perception of the police in Costa Rica tends to be **mixed**. On one hand, Costa Rica's police are generally seen as professional and dedicated to maintaining peace in the country, particularly in comparison to some other Central American nations.

The **Fuerza Pública**, as the national police, is viewed by many as responsive and helpful, especially in tourist areas, where they are tasked with ensuring the safety of visitors. The **Tourist Police**, in particular, are often praised for their friendly and approachable demeanor, which contributes to a positive perception among tourists. In urban areas, police officers are often seen as approachable and helpful in addressing everyday concerns, and there is relatively low corruption compared to regional standards.

However, there are also some **challenges to public trust**. In certain communities, particularly in marginalized or rural areas, there can be a sense of disconnection or mistrust toward the police. Issues such as **perceived corruption, police misconduct**, and the occasional use of excessive force have raised concerns, particularly in dealing with lower-income and minority communities. The growing problem of drug-related violence and organized crime in the country has led to perceptions of the police as overwhelmed or insufficiently equipped to tackle these complex issues effectively.

In recent years, Costa Rica has taken steps to improve **community policing** initiatives, with a focus on building stronger relationships between law enforcement and local communities. These reforms aim to address the distrust and create a more collaborative environment for preventing crime. However, challenges remain in improving **transparency**, ensuring **accountability**, and **addressing inequalities** in police treatment of different social groups.

Police Use of Force

Police use of force in Costa Rica is generally less of a pressing issue compared to many other Latin American countries, but it still remains a concern in certain contexts. While the country's police force is widely regarded as more professional and accountable, there are still some contexts in which police tends to use excessive force:

- **Protests and Social Unrest:** Costa Rica has experienced significant protests over issues like austerity measures and economic inequality. During these events, police have sometimes been accused of using excessive force to control crowds, with incidents of rubber bullets, tear gas, and physical violence against protestors and journalists. These actions have raised concerns about how the police handle public demonstrations.
- **Drug-Related Violence:** As a transit country for drug trafficking, Costa Rica faces challenges with organized crime. Police often

engage in confrontations with criminal groups, which can result in incidents where the use of force is called into question, especially in high-stakes drug-related operations.

- **Interactions with Marginalized Communities:** Police interactions with vulnerable groups, such as migrants from neighboring countries and indigenous communities, have occasionally sparked tensions. There have been reports of mistreatment or heavy-handed policing, particularly in areas with land disputes or environmental concerns. These situations often involve excessive force, which exacerbates community-police tensions.

 **Law of the Land True Story[35]**

On September 9, 2023, a protest against police violence in Costa Rica escalated into clashes between demonstrators and law enforcement. The protest, which began at San José's central park and proceeded to the Legislative Assembly, was sparked by recent allegations of police abuse, including an incident involving a 23-year-old woman from Alajuela. She claimed to have been assaulted, choked, and inappropriately touched by around 15 police officers outside a bar, leading to widespread outrage.

Tensions heightened at the Legislative Assembly when police attempted to remove a banner condemning police violence, resulting in confrontations. During the clash, the police detained three individuals for resisting arrest and another for vandalism. One protester was treated for injuries from a baton strike, while the police reported that several officers were injured. In response to the allegations, the Ministry of Public Security (MSP) initiated an internal investigation into the incident in Alajuela. Vice Minister Eric Lacayo expressed regret over the situation and assured that appropriate actions would be taken. The investigation is ongoing as the country grapples with concerns about police brutality.

---

35 https://ticotimes.net/2023/09/10/
    costa-rica-protest-against-police-violence-leads-to-clashes

HOW TO GET LEGAL HELP IN COSTA RICA

HOW TO GET LEGAL HELP IN COSTA RICA

Available Resources

If you find yourself in legal trouble while traveling in Costa Rica, there are several important contacts and resources you can reach out to for assistance:

Your Embassy or Consulate

The embassy or consulate of your home country can provide critical assistance if you're arrested or in legal trouble. They can help you understand your rights, connect you with local legal representation, and ensure you are treated according to international legal standards.

Find your country's embassy or consulate in Costa Rica and reach out to them immediately. They may be able to visit you, provide legal resources, or assist with translation services.

- **US Embassy:** +506 2519-2000 (or 011-506-2519-2000 from the USA)
- **Canadian Embassy:** +506 2242-4400
- **British Embassy:** +506 2258-2025

Costa Rican Bar Association (Colegio de Abogados y Abogadas de Costa Rica)

The Costa Rican Bar Association can help you find a qualified attorney if you need legal representation. They maintain a directory of licensed lawyers who can assist with various types of legal issues, including criminal, civil, or administrative cases. You can contact them for lawyer recommendations or assistance finding legal representation.

- **Website:** https://www.abogados.or.cr/
- **Phone:** +506-2253-0199

Public Defender's Office (Defensoría Pública)

If you cannot afford a lawyer, Costa Rica's Public Defender's Office offers free legal assistance to individuals who need it. This service is available for both Costa Rican nationals and foreigners who are in legal trouble. Reach out to them for help, especially if you need a lawyer for criminal or civil cases.

- **Website:** Defensoría Pública
- **Phone:** 800-DEFENSOR (800-333-3676)

Judicial Investigation Department (OIJ)

If you are involved in a criminal case, the OIJ is the primary investigative agency. If you are being accused of a crime, they can provide information on the progress of the investigation, and you can also reach out to them for clarification about criminal matters. The OIJ operates nationwide and can assist with criminal matters, investigations, or inquiries into legal cases.

- **Website:** OIJ
- **Phone:** 800-8000-645 (Emergency Number)

Private Law Firms

If you need specific legal representation and prefer private counsel, Costa Rica has many law firms specializing in criminal law, immigration law, civil disputes, or business law. If you're unsure where to start, consulting a private attorney can ensure your case is handled professionally. You can look up law firms online, or on the Costa Rican Bar Association's website which has a directory of licensed lawyers who can assist with your case.

Legal Aid

In Costa Rica, **foreign visitors are eligible for legal aid** if they are unable to afford private legal representation, especially in cases related to criminal matters or human rights violations. To qualify, individuals must demonstrate **financial need**, and the **type of case**—such as criminal defense, human rights violations, or some civil disputes—will influence eligibility.

The process begins by contacting the **Defensoría Pública** (Public Defender's Office), where applicants are assessed based on their financial situation. If approved, a public defender is assigned to represent the individual in court and offer legal advice. Legal aid may also cover court fees and provide translation services if needed. However, private legal representation, travel costs, and personal expenses are not typically covered under legal aid.

Although legal aid is available to foreigners, the type of case and residency status may affect eligibility, with priority often given to cases involving fundamental rights. Overall, the legal aid system in Costa Rica is designed to ensure that all individuals, regardless of their financial status, have access to fair legal representation when facing legal challenges.

Foreign Embassies in Costa Rica

The **primary role** of an embassy or consulate is to **represent and protect the interests of their home country and its citizens in a foreign country**. This includes providing consular services such as issuing passports, assisting with visas, offering support in emergencies (e.g., medical, legal, or travel issues), and helping citizens who are arrested or detained. Additionally, embassies and consulates foster diplomatic relations between countries, engage in trade and cultural exchanges, and provide information about the home country's policies, laws, and services. The embassy typically handles more significant diplomatic affairs, while consulates manage more localized services and support for citizens.

As of recent information, Costa Rica hosts approximately **50 foreign embassies** and around **15 consulates.** These diplomatic missions represent various countries and provide a wide range of services, such as visa issuance, consular assistance, and promoting trade and cultural exchanges between their home countries and Costa Rica.

Embassies are typically located in the capital, **San José**, while **consulates** may be found in other major cities like **Liberia** or **Puntarenas**. Some countries maintain both an embassy and consulates in Costa Rica, depending on their diplomatic and consular needs.

For the most up-to-date information, you can refer to the **Ministry of Foreign Affairs and Worship of Costa Rica** or check directly with the embassy or consulate you are interested in. Here is contact information for some of the biggest embassies in Costa Rica:

United States Embassy

+506 2519-2000

https://cr.usembassy.gov

Canada Embassy

+506 2242-4400

https://www.canadainternational.gc.ca/costarica

Mexico Embassy

+506 2242-4400

https://embamex.sre.gob.mx/costarica

Spain Embassy

+506 2220-3500

http://www.exteriores.gob.es/embajadas/sanjose

United Kingdom Embassy

+506 2258-2025

https://www.gov.uk/world/organisations/british-embassy-san-jose

CHAPTER 17

MEDICAL FACILITIES & HOSPITALS

IN THIS CHAPTER

- Overview
- Visitors' Access to Healthcare in Costa Rica
- Costa Rican Hospitals
- Medical Emergencies
- Insurance Guidance

MEDICAL FACILITIES & HOSPITALS

Overview

Costa Rica is renowned for having **one of the most effective and high-quality healthcare systems in Latin America**. The country offers a comprehensive mix of public and private services that ensures its residents and visitors have access to excellent medical care. The healthcare system is designed to be both accessible and affordable, emphasizing preventive care, affordability, and high standards of medical treatment.

At the core of Costa Rica's healthcare system is the **Caja Costarricense de Seguro Social** (CCSS), which provides **universal healthcare coverage** to all legal residents, including both citizens and expatriates. Funded primarily through payroll contributions from employees and employers—typically ranging from 9% to 11% of an individual's salary—the public system offers a wide range of services, such as general medical care, hospitalizations, surgeries, and emergency care. Legal residents must enroll in the CCSS program, which allows them to access public healthcare services across the country. The system is designed to ensure that healthcare is available to everyone, regardless of income.

Primary healthcare is typically provided through **EBAIS clinics**, which are local healthcare teams that offer services such as routine check-ups, vaccinations, and preventive care. Patients who require specialized care can be referred to larger public hospitals, often located in urban centers like San José. These public hospitals are well-equipped and provide quality care but wait times for non-emergency services can sometimes be long due to high demand. Despite this, the system remains an essential and affordable option for most of the population.

Alongside the public system, Costa Rica also boasts a thriving **private healthcare sector**. Private hospitals and clinics in the country are often equipped with state-of-the-art technology and staffed by highly trained medical professionals. Many doctors have studied abroad, and English-speaking staff are common in private facilities, making this sector particularly attractive to expatriates and medical tourists. Private healthcare offers quicker access to specialists, shorter waiting times, and more personalized attention, although services are generally more expensive than those provided by the public system. The private sector is often chosen by those who need more immediate treatment or prefer a higher level of comfort and convenience.

For expatriates, accessing healthcare in Costa Rica is relatively simple. After becoming a legal resident, individuals must register with the CCSS and contribute to the public system. Residents can also opt for private health insurance, which provides access to private healthcare facilities and may cover services not fully reimbursed by the public system. Private insurance is particularly useful for those who want faster access to medical care or prefer a higher level of service.

The medical professionals in Costa Rica are highly regarded. Many doctors have received training in renowned institutions in the United States or Europe, and the **Colegio de Médicos y Cirujanos**, Costa Rica's medical licensing board, ensures that healthcare providers adhere to high standards. English-speaking doctors are readily available, particularly in private hospitals, making it easier for expatriates to communicate and navigate the healthcare system.

Pharmaceuticals in Costa Rica are widely available, with both prescription and over-the-counter medications offered at lower prices than in many other countries. While controlled substances do require a prescription, many common medications can be purchased without one. Pharmacies are common throughout the country, even in smaller towns, so residents and visitors typically have easy access to the medications they need.

Visitors' Access to Healthcare in Costa Rica

One of the most common ways for visitors to access healthcare in Costa Rica is by using **travel insurance** that includes medical coverage. Many travelers purchase travel insurance before their trip, which can cover a wide range of medical services, from hospital stays to emergency medical evacuation. Travel insurance is particularly important if you're planning to engage in outdoor activities or adventure tourism, where the risk of injury could be higher. It is essential to ensure that the policy covers health services specifically in Costa Rica and provides adequate coverage for both emergency and non-emergency medical care. Some international travel insurance plans also cover repatriation costs should you need to return to your home country for treatment.

In addition to traditional travel insurance, visitors can also purchase **short-term private health insurance**, which is available through a variety of local providers. These plans are tailored for non-residents and tourists, covering emergency services, hospital stays, and sometimes outpatient treatments. This is a good option if you're planning to stay for a longer period and want to ensure you're covered for any potential health issues during your time in the country. Private health insurance options typically offer faster access to medical services and fewer bureaucratic hurdles than the public system.

Visitors to Costa Rica can also pay **out-of-pocket** for medical services. Healthcare in Costa Rica, both in public and private facilities, is much more affordable than in many countries, particularly the U.S. and Europe. For example, a visit to a private doctor might cost between US$50 to $100, while more specialized treatments like surgery or dental procedures may be a fraction of the price they would cost in North America. While this is often the most straightforward option for tourists without insurance, it's important to know that costs can vary depending on the facility and the treatment you require. In private hospitals and clinics, you'll usually pay upfront for medical services and will receive an invoice for your records.

Costa Rica has become a popular destination for **medical tourism**, particularly for procedures such as dental work, cosmetic surgery, and orthopedic treatments. Many private hospitals and clinics cater specifically to international patients. They offer a range of elective and non-elective procedures at competitive rates, with some even providing packages that include accommodations and transport. If you're coming to Costa Rica for medical treatment, many facilities will handle much of the logistics for you, from arranging doctor consultations to organizing transportation to and from the hospital.

Costa Rican Hospitals

Costa Rica's healthcare system stands out for its broad coverage and accessibility, playing a vital role in maintaining the nation's public health. As of January 23, 2025, the country has approximately **172 hospitals**, which include both public and private institutions that serve the country's population of about five million people.[36] This extensive network of healthcare facilities, combined with one of the highest ratios of doctors and nurses per capita in Central America, highlights the country's strong healthcare workforce committed to meeting the needs of its citizens.

The distribution of healthcare facilities across Costa Rica is not uniform, with the **majority of hospitals** and medical services concentrated in the capital city, **San José**. Key private hospitals, such as **Hospital CIMA** and **Hospital Clínica Bíblica**, are located in this urban area, which serves as the healthcare hub of the country. While the public healthcare system has a presence in various provinces like Limón, Puntarenas, Alajuela, and Cartago, access to healthcare can be uneven, creating disparities between urban and rural areas.[37]

The **public healthcare system**, managed by the *Caja Costarricense de Seguro Social* (CCSS), operates **15 public hospitals** throughout the country. In addition to these hospitals, the system provides primary care services through a network of **EBAIS** (outpatient clinics and health centers) that are located in communities nationwide. Although efforts

---

36 https://rentechdigital.com/smartscraper/business-report-details/
list-of-hospitals-in-costa-rica

37 https://crie.cr/what-are-the-best-hospitals-in-costa-rica/

are made to ensure healthcare services are accessible in both urban and rural regions, the concentration of resources in cities like San José continues to present challenges for residents in more remote areas. This geographical imbalance underscores the ongoing need for investment in healthcare infrastructure to ensure equal access to services across the country.

Most Prominent Hospitals

Among the most significant **public hospitals** under the CCSS umbrella are *Hospital San Juan de Dios*, *Hospital México*, and *Hospital Calderón Guardia*, all of which are located in the capital city of San José. These hospitals are crucial in serving a large portion of the population, offering a broad range of medical services at no direct cost to patients who are enrolled in the CAJA system.

For international visitors seeking healthcare in a more comfortable and personalized setting, **private hospitals** in Costa Rica are particularly attractive. **Hospital CIMA**, located in San José, is frequently regarded as the best hospital for travelers and expatriates.[38] Known for meeting international standards, it is equipped with cutting-edge medical technology and staffed by professionals trained to assist foreign patients. The hospital offers a full range of specialized services, including cardiology and orthopedics, making it a preferred option for those seeking advanced treatments.

Another prominent private facility is **Hospital Clínica Bíblica**, which has been serving patients since 1929. As the largest private hospital in Costa Rica, it has earned a reputation for exceptional care and modern medical services. The hospital's commitment to quality healthcare, coupled with its English-speaking staff, makes it particularly well-suited for international visitors. Likewise, **Hospital La Católica**, located in Guadalupe, San José, also offers high-quality healthcare at affordable prices. Known for its friendly atmosphere and attentive service, this

---

38 https://www.flyreva.com/blog/best-international-hospitals-in-the-world/
   best-international-hospitals-hospitals-in-costa-rica/

facility is a popular choice for surgical procedures, which tend to be more costly in other regions.

While Costa Rica does not have hospitals officially classified as "American hospitals," several private facilities have strong ties to the U.S. healthcare system. **Hospital CIMA**, for example, is operated by a Texas-based group and is especially favored by North Americans due to its adherence to familiar hospital practices and standards.[39] Many of the doctors at these facilities have received training in the United States and are fluent in English, which makes communication easier for international patients. Similarly, **Hospital Clínica Bíblica** maintains partnerships with several respected U.S. institutions, integrating international standards into its operations.[40] This connection with American medical institutions further bolsters its appeal among foreign patients seeking high-quality care in Costa Rica.

Medical Emergencies

1. **What should you do if you feel unwell/sick in Costa Rica?** If you feel unwell or sick in Costa Rica, the first step is to assess the severity of your symptoms. For minor ailments, you can visit a local EBAIS clinic for basic medical attention. These community-based health centers provide general care and are available throughout the country. In more serious cases or if you require specialized care, you can go to a private clinic or hospital. Private hospitals, such as Hospital CIMA or Hospital Clínica Bíblica, offer quick access to English-speaking doctors and advanced treatment

---

39 https://www.gaprealestate.com/
    are-there-good-private-hospitals-in-costa-rica/

40 https://www.flyreva.com/blog/best-international-hospitals-in-the-world/
    best-international-hospitals-hospitals-in-costa-rica/

options. It's also a good idea to have travel insurance or private health insurance in case you need medical services.

2. **What if you need hospital care in Costa Rica?** If you need hospital care in Costa Rica, you have a few options depending on the situation. For emergency care, you can go to a public hospital such as Hospital San Juan de Dios or Hospital México, where treatment will be provided at no direct cost if you are enrolled in the national insurance system (CAJA). If you prefer a private hospital, Hospital CIMA or Hospital Clínica Bíblica offer specialized services and are equipped with advanced technology, though you will need to pay out-of-pocket or through insurance. Depending on the seriousness of your condition, emergency rooms and outpatient services are available, and English-speaking staff are common in private hospitals.

 Here are the most important emergency numbers you should place in your phone while in Costa Rica:

- **Emergency (Police, Fire, Ambulance):** 911
- **Police:** 112
- **Fire Department:** 118
- **Ambulance:** 128
- **Red Cross (Cruz Roja):** 132

Insurance Guidance[41]

Foreign insurance plans are **generally accepted** in Costa Rica, especially in private hospitals and clinics. Many private facilities work with international insurance providers. If you have travel insurance or international health insurance, you can typically file a claim for medical

---

41 https://www.internations.org/costa-rica-expats/guide/healthcare

expenses. However, it's important to confirm that your insurance covers services in Costa Rica before you seek care, as not all foreign plans may cover all medical services abroad. Some hospitals may require you to pay upfront and later reimburse you, so it's advisable to check with the hospital and your insurer beforehand.

The costs of medical services in Costa Rica are generally much lower than in the U.S. or Europe. Here are some average prices for common medical services:

- **Emergency Room (ER) Visit:** US$50–$150 (depending on the severity)
- **Doctor's Visit (Private clinic):** US$50–$100
- **Specialist Consultation:** US$100–$200
- **Dental Consultation:** US$30–$50
- **Minor Surgery (e.g., small procedures):** US$500–$1,500

The cost can vary depending on the facility, the location (private vs. public), and the type of treatment.

How Do You Pay?

Public Healthcare: If you're covered by Costa Rica's CAJA system, there is no direct payment for services at public hospitals and clinics (as it is included in your insurance contributions).

Private Healthcare: For private healthcare, you can pay out-of-pocket or use your private insurance. Payment is typically due at the time of service. Major credit cards are widely accepted, and some hospitals may allow direct billing to foreign insurance providers if pre-approved.

DRIVING IN COSTA RICA

DRIVING IN COSTA RICA

Overview

Driving in Costa Rica can be an exciting yet challenging experience, especially for those not accustomed to the country's road conditions and driving style. In general, Costa Rica has a reputation for having a more relaxed approach to traffic laws, and the driving culture can feel **chaotic** at times, particularly in urban areas like San José. Drivers often display a mix of courtesy and impatience, and aggressive driving, such as frequent lane changes and tailgating, is common. However, locals tend to be helpful to tourists, often offering directions if you get lost.

Traffic congestion is a significant issue in larger cities, especially during rush hour. The streets in San José can be particularly crowded, with long delays due to poorly coordinated traffic signals and street maintenance projects. In contrast, driving in rural areas and smaller towns is typically more relaxed, although roads can be narrow and winding, especially in the mountainous regions.

Tourists may also encounter challenges such as **poor signage** in some areas, **fewer traffic lights**, and **unfamiliar driving practices**. Speeding is generally not enforced as strictly as in other countries, but road conditions—such as potholes, unpredictable weather, and unmarked obstacles—can pose risks.

Costa Rica's **road infrastructure** is a mix of well-maintained highways, rural roads, and less-developed routes. The **Inter-American Highway**, which runs through the country, is the primary route connecting major cities and regions, and it's generally in good condition. However, the quality of roads varies significantly outside urban centers.

Major highways, especially those near San José, Liberia, and Alajuela, are paved and **well-maintained**, though you may encounter occasional potholes or rough patches. The road network connecting popular tourist destinations, such as Arenal Volcano or Manuel Antonio, is generally functional but may not be as smooth or wide as highways in developed countries.

Secondary and rural roads are often in **poor condition**, with many being narrow, winding, and sometimes unpaved. During the rainy season (May to November), flooding and mudslides can make rural roads particularly treacherous. Mountainous regions and remote areas, such as the Nicoya Peninsula or the Osa Peninsula, often feature gravel roads that can be challenging to navigate, especially for inexperienced drivers.

Road signage can be inconsistent, particularly in rural areas. While major roads are usually clearly marked, secondary roads may have limited or confusing signage. Drivers are advised to use GPS or maps to avoid getting lost.

Frequent roadwork and construction projects are common in Costa Rica. While roads are often improved, this can lead to delays and detours. It's important to drive cautiously and stay alert to changing road conditions.

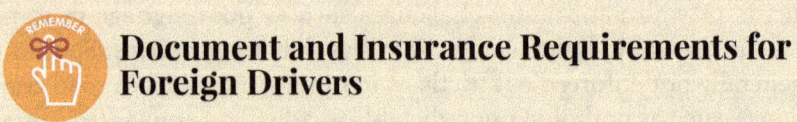

Document and Insurance Requirements for Foreign Drivers

Foreign drivers in Costa Rica must meet certain requirements to legally operate a vehicle:

- **Valid Driver's License:** You can drive in Costa Rica with a foreign driver's license for up to 90 days as a tourist. After this period, you may need to obtain a Costa Rican driver's license if you plan to stay longer. It is recommended that you carry an International Driving Permit (IDP) along with your home country's driver's license, as it can help if you need to communicate with authorities. However, an IDP is not required if your license is in English.

- **Vehicle Registration and Proof of Insurance:** Whether you rent or bring your own vehicle, you must have the vehicle's registration and proof of insurance with you. If you rent a car, the rental agency will provide these documents. For private vehicles, the registration document should be kept in the car, along with proof of liability insurance.

- **Car Insurance (Mandatory):** It is mandatory to have at least liability insurance to drive in Costa Rica. Most car rental companies will offer insurance as part of the rental agreement, but make sure you confirm that collision, theft, and liability coverage are included. If you have personal auto insurance, check with your provider to see if it covers driving in Costa Rica.

- **Rental Car Insurance:** If renting, third-party insurance (often referred to as SOAT, or Seguro Obligatorio de Accidentes de Tránsito) is mandatory and typically included in the rental fee, but additional coverage for collision or theft may be offered at extra cost.

 ## Main Traffic Rules

- **Driving side:** Vehicles drive on the right side of the road.

- **Speed limits:** Urban areas 25-40 km/h (15-25 mph), secondary roads 40-60 km/h (25-37 mph), highways 80-100 km/h (50-62 mph).

- **Seat belts:** Mandatory for all passengers in the front and rear seats.

- **Alcohol:** The legal BAC limit is 0.02%, with strict penalties for DUI.

- **Mobile devices:** Use of mobile phones is prohibited while driving unless hands-free.

- **Toll roads:** Tolls are paid in cash or via a prepaid pass.

- **If stopped by police:** Stay calm, provide documents, and avoid bribery.

- **Road safety:** Be mindful of poor road conditions, especially in the rainy season.

Some Unique Traffic Rules

Driving in Costa Rica involves a few unique signals and customs that visitors should be aware of. For example, **flashing headlights** is a common practice on highways, particularly in rural areas. Drivers often use this signal to indicate it's safe to pass, or to show appreciation for someone letting them through.

An unusual but accepted practice in Costa Rica is the ability to **turn left at a red light**, unless otherwise indicated by a sign. This might catch visitors off guard but is a routine part of local driving. Pedestrian rights are taken seriously, and drivers are expected to stop for pedestrians at designated crosswalks. That said, it's not uncommon for pedestrians to cross outside of these areas, especially in busy urban environments.

Additionally, **speed bumps**—known as *topes*—are widespread in Costa Rica, particularly in residential neighborhoods and smaller towns. These bumps are often not well-marked, so drivers need to stay alert to avoid damaging their vehicles. Finally, in more rural or less regulated areas, there may be **unofficial "yield" signs** at intersections, where traffic from the right typically has the right of way, even in the absence of formal signage. Drivers should always proceed with caution in these areas to navigate safely.

General Questions

1. *Can I use my driver's license from my home country to drive in Costa Rica?* **Yes.** You can use your driver's license from your home country to drive in Costa Rica for up to 90 days as a tourist. However, it's recommended to also carry an International Driving Permit (IDP), especially if your license is not in Spanish.

2. *What is the age requirement for renting a car in Costa Rica?* The minimum age to rent a car in Costa Rica is typically **21 years old**, though some rental agencies may require drivers to be at least 25 or impose a young driver fee for those under 25.

Law of the Land Hypothetical

HYPOTHETICAL: *Sarah, a tourist from the United States, has been traveling through Costa Rica for a week. She rented a car and is driving from San José to the beach. While driving on a rural road, she accidentally goes over a speed bump too quickly and her car's rear suspension gets damaged. She pulls over to assess the damage, but a police officer stops to check on her. The officer informs her that she was speeding before the incident and issues a fine. Sarah explains that she was unaware of the speed limit in the area and didn't see any speed signs. Is Sarah responsible for paying the fine, even though she claims she did not see the speed limit signs and was unaware of the limit?*

ANSWER: **Yes.** *Sarah is still responsible for paying the fine. In Costa Rica, as in many countries, drivers are expected to be aware of and follow local traffic laws, regardless of whether they see specific speed limit signs. Ignorance of the law is generally not accepted as an excuse for breaking it. Additionally, speed limits in rural areas can be difficult to notice if they are not clearly marked, but drivers are still expected to drive cautiously and within reasonable limits. In this case, even if*

Sarah didn't see any speed limit signs, she could be held accountable for the infraction if the officer determined she was speeding.

NUDE BEACHES & CLOTHING-OPTIONAL RESORTS

NUDE BEACHES & CLOTHING-OPTIONAL RESORTS

Overview

Nudism in Costa Rica is **not widely accepted** as part of the mainstream culture, as the country tends to have more conservative attitudes toward public nudity. However, there are certain areas, particularly private beaches and resorts, where nudism is more tolerated. For example, some remote beaches, like those in the Nicoya Peninsula and on the Pacific coast, are known to attract nudists, though they are generally not officially designated as clothing optional. Public nudity is **generally prohibited by law**, and local customs discourage nudism in most public places.

There are, however, a few **hotels and resorts** in Costa Rica that **cater to naturist or clothing-optional guests**. These establishments provide a more relaxed, private environment where nudism is permitted. Among more prominent establishments are:

- **Hotel Punta Islita:** Located on the Nicoya Peninsula, this hotel is known for its secluded atmosphere and beautiful natural surroundings. While not strictly a "naturist" hotel, it offers private, clothing-optional areas for guests looking for a more relaxed and discreet experience.

- **Villas Río Mar:** Situated near Dominical on the Pacific Coast, this boutique hotel is known to offer clothing-optional accommodations and spaces, including private villas and pools, catering to those looking for a more laid-back, naturist friendly experience.

- **The Harmony Hotel:** Located in Nosara, this eco-friendly hotel is more liberal about allowing nudity in certain private spaces, particularly around its tranquil gardens and secluded beach. While it is not exclusively a naturist resort, it has a reputation for being accepting of guests who prefer clothing-optional settings in private areas.

While not widespread, these niche accommodations can be found in some areas that attract more international tourism, where there is greater demand for such experiences. Despite this, visitors should be aware that nudism outside of these private spaces is not culturally common, and discretion is advised when exploring less-touristed areas.

Legality and Safety

Nudism is not legally recognized or specifically regulated, but local laws against public indecency and exposure apply. Public nudity is considered an offense under public indecency laws. Penalties can include fines, arrest, or detention, especially if the nudity is disruptive or offensive. More serious charges could apply if the act is linked to other offenses. While some remote beaches may attract naturists, public nudity outside of designated private spaces can lead to fines or even legal action.

Regarding nudist etiquette, it's important to be respectful and discreet. When staying at a clothing-optional hotel or resort, always follow the rules and respect the boundaries of other guests. Public nudity is usually only acceptable in specific, private areas (like a designated pool or beach area), and guests should avoid nudity in public spaces, such as restaurants or walking through public areas. If you're unsure whether nudism is acceptable in a particular area, it's best to err on the side of caution and keep your clothes on. Always be respectful of local culture and customs, as nudism is not a widespread practice in Costa Rican society.

Safety should always be a priority, and you should consider the following factors:

1. **Research the Destination:** Look for established nudist beaches or resorts with good reviews. Online forums and social media can provide insights from fellow travelers about safety and experiences.

2. **Local Regulations:** Familiarize yourself with the rules of the specific beach or resort. Some places may have designated areas for nudism, while others might be more lenient. Adhering to local customs helps ensure a positive experience.

3. **Travel in Groups:** If possible, visit with friends or fellow travelers. There's safety in numbers, and it can enhance the experience to share it with others.

4. **Stay Aware of Your Surroundings:** As with any beach or resort, it's wise to be aware of your environment. Keep personal belongings secure and be cautious of anyone acting suspiciously.

5. **Trust Your Instincts:** If a place feels uncomfortable or unwelcoming, it's okay to leave and seek another location.

6. **Respect Others' Privacy:** Nudist communities value consent and privacy. Always be respectful of others and avoid taking photos without permission.

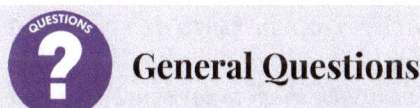

General Questions

1. *Are there specific beaches or remote spots in Costa Rica that are well-known for nudism, and what should I know before visiting them?* **Yes.** Costa Rica has no official nudist beaches, but remote spots like Playa Hermosa and Playa Barrigona are known for attracting nudists. Public nudity elsewhere can lead to legal issues, so always be discreet and respectful of local customs.

2. *What should I wear when visiting a nude beach in Costa Rica, and is it necessary to bring anything specific?* On a nude beach, nudity is expected but bring a cover-up for walking to and from the beach. Essentials include sunscreen, a towel, water, and possibly a hat. Check specific beach rules, as some may have additional guidelines.

 **Law of the Land Hypothetical**

HYPOTHETICAL: *John and Lisa, a couple from Canada, are staying at a clothing-optional resort in Costa Rica. They've been enjoying the private beach area where nudism is permitted. One day, while walking along the beach near the resort, they encounter a couple of local tourists who are fully clothed and seem uncomfortable with their nudity. The locals approach John and Lisa and ask them to put clothes on, stating they are offended by the sight. John and Lisa argue that they are on a clothing-optional beach and aren't breaking any rules. However, the locals call the police, claiming the couple is violating public decency laws. Are John and Lisa at risk of legal trouble for walking nude on a public beach near their clothing-optional resort?*

ANSWER: *While the resort may allow nudity on its private property, public beaches outside of designated clothing-optional areas may have different rules. In Costa Rica, public nudity is generally illegal, and if John and Lisa are outside the resort's private property and the beach is considered a public space, they could face legal penalties for public indecency. The police may issue a fine or ask them to cover up. To avoid legal trouble, it's important to stay within the designated private areas of the resort and not venture into public spaces while nude.*

UNUSUAL LAWS

UNUSUAL LAWS

Overview

Unusual laws can be fascinating glimpses into a culture's values and history. While most people are aware of common legal restrictions, it's often the strange and quirky laws that capture our attention. These regulations can range from the amusing to the absurd, reflecting the unique circumstances and traditions of a place. Whether they arise from historical events, societal norms, or simply peculiar local customs, unusual laws can provide insight into the quirks of human behavior and governance.

 **Costa Rica's Unusual Laws and Associated Penalties**

Like any country, Costa Rica has a set of unique and sometimes quirky laws that might surprise visitors. While most of these laws are rooted in cultural traditions, historical practices, or attempts to protect public safety, they can still lead to confusion or unintended legal trouble if not understood. Understanding these laws, along with the penalties for breaking them, can help travelers navigate the country smoothly and avoid any unwelcome surprises during their stay. From outdated regulations on dueling to unusual rules about animals wearing shoes, Costa Rica's legal landscape is filled with peculiarities:

- **No Dueling:** Dueling, even if it's a friendly challenge, is illegal in Costa Rica. This dates back to old colonial times when dueling was a common practice among the upper class. Engaging in a duel can result in **criminal charges**, including imprisonment.

- **Shoe Laws for Animals:** It's technically illegal to walk an animal, particularly a dog, without shoes. This law was created to protect animals' paws from being harmed by the hot pavement in urban areas. While rarely enforced, breaking this quirky law could lead to **a fine** or a **warning** from animal control officers.

- **No Liquor Sales on Specific Holidays:** In Costa Rica, the sale of alcohol is prohibited on certain holidays like Good Friday, Independence Day, and other religious or national observances. Violating this law could result in **fines** or a **temporary closure** of the establishment caught selling alcohol.

- **Traffic Laws with Odd Requirements:** All vehicles must have a reflective triangle or emergency warning device in the car at all times, even for short trips. If caught without the triangle during a police check, you may face **a fine** or be forced to purchase one on the spot.

- **The Absence of "No Smoking" Signs:** There is a unique law that prohibits smoking in places that do not display "No Smoking" signs. Smokers who violate this law can face fines or be asked to leave the premises.

- **No Public Dancing After 10 PM:** In some areas of Costa Rica, it's prohibited to engage in public dancing after 10 PM to prevent noise disturbances, especially in residential areas. The penalty may include a **fine** or an **order to stop the dancing**.

General Questions

1. *Is it illegal to drive with a broken windshield in Costa Rica?*
   Yes. Driving with a broken windshield **is illegal** in Costa Rica.
   According to traffic laws, a vehicle must be in good working
   condition, and a damaged windshield that obstructs the driver's
   view can lead to fines or the vehicle being deemed unroadworthy
   until repaired.

2. *Can you be fined for not using your vehicle's turn signals
   in Costa Rica?* **Yes**. Failing to use your turn signals is a traffic
   violation in Costa Rica. The penalty can include a fine, and more
   importantly, it could be dangerous as it increases the risk of
   accidents.

3. *Are there laws regarding the use of drones in Costa Rica?* **Yes**.
   Costa Rica has specific laws regarding drone use. Drones are regulated by the Costa Rican Civil Aviation Authority (DGAC), and
   to fly a drone commercially or in certain public areas, you must
   obtain a permit. Unauthorized drone use in restricted areas, such
   as near airports or national parks, can result in fines or confiscation of the drone.

 **Law of the Land Hypothetical**

HYPOTHETICAL: *Anna, a tourist visiting Costa Rica, is exploring the city of San José. While walking around, she notices a beautiful view of the city from a park and decides to take some photos with her drone. After flying the drone for about 15 minutes, a park ranger approaches her and informs her that drone use is not allowed in the area without proper authorization. Anna argues that she was just taking some personal photos and didn't know about the restriction. Did Anna break any laws by flying her drone in the park without authorization, and what are the possible consequences?*

ANSWER: **Yes.** *Anna violated Costa Rica's drone regulations by flying in a public park without authorization. Drones are restricted in certain areas, including national parks and urban spaces, unless the operator has a permit. She could face a fine or drone confiscation. Anna should have checked for local restrictions or obtained a permit beforehand.*

CHAPTER 21

TRAVELING SAFELY

IN THIS CHAPTER

- Ladies Traveling Solo
- Traveling as a Family
- Advice for All Travelers
- Do's and Don'ts While in Costa Rica

CHAPTER 21

TRAVELING SAFELY

Ladies Traveling Solo

Costa Rica has a reputation for being a peaceful and welcoming country with a focus on sustainability and eco-tourism. It is often considered a top destination for solo travelers due to its friendly locals, beautiful landscapes, and rich biodiversity. Many tourists — including solo female travelers — visit Costa Rica each year without encountering any major issues. The country has a stable political environment and is recognized for its high levels of safety in comparison to neighboring countries.

Nevertheless, it's important to take a few precautions to ensure a safe and enjoyable trip. One of the most common issues solo travelers face, regardless of gender, is **petty theft**. In busy places like San José, the capital, or at popular tourist sites, pickpocketing and bag snatching can be a problem. It's wise to keep your belongings secure and avoid flaunting expensive items like jewelry or electronics in public, as they can attract unwanted attention.

Costa Rica's natural beauty draws visitors to its remote areas, including rainforests, beaches, and volcanoes. For solo adventurers, these areas offer incredible opportunities for hiking, biking, and exploration, but it's important to plan carefully. Before setting out on your own, do some research on the trails or locations you intend to visit. If you're heading into more isolated areas, it's a good idea to consider joining a guided tour to ensure your safety. Some coastal regions, in particular, can have a higher risk of opportunistic crime, though violent crime against tourists remains rare.

When it comes to **transportation**, Costa Rica offers public buses and taxis, but it's best to use established companies for both. Be cautious about accepting rides from strangers, especially in less populated areas. If you're traveling to remote destinations, renting a car or using a reliable shuttle service may be a safer and more convenient option.

Costa Rica is known for its adventure tourism, offering activities like surfing, zip-lining, and hiking. While these experiences are exciting, they also come with risks. To stay safe, always **opt for certified guides** who adhere to safety regulations and double-check that any equipment you'll be using is in good condition.

As for cultural attitudes, Costa Ricans, or "Ticos," are generally friendly, warm, and welcoming to visitors. The country also has a relatively **low incidence of gender-based violence** compared to many other parts of the world. However, as with any destination, it's essential to be mindful of your personal space, especially in less touristy or poorly lit areas. Avoid walking alone at night, particularly in places where you may feel uncomfortable or unsafe.

By staying aware of your surroundings and following these simple precautions, you can enjoy all the beauty and adventure that Costa Rica has to offer while feeling confident and secure as a solo female traveler.

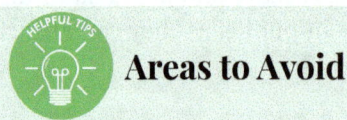

Areas to Avoid

There are certain areas where solo female travelers should be more cautious. In **San José**, the capital, neighborhoods like **La Carpio**, **El Carmen**, and **Pavas** are known for higher crime rates, especially petty theft. It's best to stick to safer areas like **Escazú** or **Avenida Central** during the day and avoid wandering around at night.

On the Caribbean Coast, Puerto Limón and some of the more remote areas have higher levels of crime, so it's advisable to stay vigilant, especially after dark. For a safer experience, focus on more popular tourist spots like **Cahuita** and **Puerto Viejo.**

In **Guanacaste**, while towns like **Tamarindo** are generally safe, more isolated beaches and quieter parts of the region can attract opportunistic criminals. Stick to well-reviewed accommodations and be mindful of your valuables, especially when visiting remote beaches.

In **Alajuela**, while the area near the international airport is safe, neighborhoods such as **La Fortuna** can experience street crime. It's best to avoid walking alone after dark and to use reputable transport options.

Some **coastal areas**, particularly those that are more isolated, can be risky at night. To stay safe, opt for popular, well-lit beach towns like **Jaco** or **Manuel Antonio** after sunset.

Finally, on the **Nicoya Peninsula**, certain remote parts, especially in the north, may be less safe. It's best to stick to known spots like **Nosara** or **Playa Samara**, which are more frequented by tourists and generally safer.

By staying in well-populated areas, using trusted services, and avoiding remote spots after dark, solo female travelers can enjoy Costa Rica's beauty with greater peace of mind.

 For some insights from ladies traveling solo to Costa Rica, visit **https://www.girlabouttheglobe.com/solo-travel-in-costa-rica/ or https://www.thefearlesswanderess.com/destinations/central-america/ solo-female-travel-to-costa-rica/.**

Traveling as a Family

Traveling with children in Costa Rica can be a fantastic experience, offering everything from lush rainforests to beautiful beaches and incredible wildlife. However, as with any family vacation, there are safety precautions to consider, particularly in a tropical country like Costa Rica. By being mindful of certain factors, you can help ensure that your trip is both enjoyable and safe for your little ones.

First and foremost, when traveling with children, **road safety** is a top priority. The roads in Costa Rica, especially in rural areas, can be rough, winding, and sometimes poorly maintained. Driving in more remote areas might require a 4x4 vehicle. If you plan to rent a car, make sure it's equipped for the terrain you'll be exploring. Children under 12 are required by law to use a child safety seat, so don't forget to arrange for one in advance. Whether you're walking around cities like San José or exploring quieter towns, always be cautious around traffic, as pedestrians don't always have the right of way.

When venturing into the country's famous natural areas, the **wildlife** is both a draw and a potential risk. Costa Rica's rainforests, jungles, and coastal areas are teeming with wildlife, including snakes, spiders, and insects. While most of these creatures aren't harmful if left alone, you'll want to keep a watchful eye on your children, particularly when hiking or exploring in the wild. Be sure to teach them not to touch plants, insects, or animals, and keep a safe distance from them. A good rule of thumb is to always supervise them closely, especially in areas where wildlife is more abundant, like national parks or reserves.

If you plan to spend time on Costa Rica's beautiful beaches, keep in mind that some of the surf can be quite strong, especially on the Pacific side. Strong currents and riptides are common in many areas, so it's important to **always swim in designated areas** that are patrolled by lifeguards. Never leave young children unattended near the water, and make sure they're always supervised during water activities. For other adventure activities, like zip-lining or rafting, ensure that the tour operators follow strict safety protocols and that the activities are suitable for children's age and abilities.

One of the most important aspects of **personal security** for children, anywhere in the world, is constant supervision. In Costa Rica, whether you're in bustling cities like San José or on remote beaches, it's essential to keep your children within sight at all times. Tourist areas, public markets, and beaches can sometimes attract opportunistic criminals, so be extra vigilant in these crowded places. If you're in a busy area, such as a market or a popular attraction, make sure your children are always close by, and talk to them about the importance of staying close and not wandering off.

To keep everyone comfortable, always have a **first-aid kit** with essential items, including band-aids, antiseptic wipes, and medications for common ailments like headaches or stomach issues. It's also a good idea to carry any prescriptions your children may need, as pharmacies may not always carry certain medications in smaller towns.

Costa Rica offers a wealth of family-friendly activities, from wildlife watching and volcano tours to zip-lining and beach days. However, it's important to pace yourselves and not over-schedule. Children, especially younger ones, need time to rest and recharge. Keep in mind that some activities, such as long hikes or intense tours, may not be suitable for younger kids or toddlers. Be sure to check age restrictions or recommendations before booking any tours or excursions.

Lastly, while Costa Rica has good medical care in major cities like San José and Liberia, in more remote areas, healthcare facilities may be limited. Having **travel insurance** that covers medical emergencies is always a good idea when traveling with children. Know the location of the nearest hospital or clinic in case of emergencies.

Advice for All Travelers

When traveling to Costa Rica, there are several important health considerations to keep in mind to ensure a safe and enjoyable trip.

First, it's important to check with your healthcare provider to ensure that your **vaccinations** are up to date before traveling. The CDC recommends vaccines for Hepatitis A, Hepatitis B, Typhoid, and Tetanus, particularly if you're planning to visit rural areas or travel outside major tourist regions. If your travels take you to the Caribbean side or near the Panamanian border, you may also need the Yellow Fever vaccine.

Costa Rica's tropical climate means that **mosquitoes** are common, and diseases like dengue and Zika are present. To protect yourself, use DEET-based insect repellents, and wear long sleeves and pants in areas with high mosquito activity such as rainforests or rural regions. If you're staying in more remote accommodations or the jungle, consider using mosquito nets over sleeping areas for added protection.

The sun in Costa Rica can be intense, so it's crucial to take **sun protection** seriously. Apply sunscreen with at least SPF 30 regularly, especially after swimming or sweating. Use wide-brimmed hats, sunglasses, and protective clothing, particularly during midday when the sun's rays are strongest.

In terms of **water safety**, tap water is generally safe to drink in urban and tourist areas. However, in rural or remote regions, it's best to stick to bottled water to avoid potential stomach issues. Be cautious with street food, as hygiene standards may vary. To reduce the risk of food-borne illnesses, avoid consuming raw or undercooked foods and choose well-established restaurants.

If you're visiting higher-altitude locations like Monteverde or Arenal, be aware that **altitude sickness** can occur, particularly if you're not acclimated. Allow yourself time to adjust, stay hydrated, and avoid overexerting yourself during the first couple of days at high elevations.

By keeping these health considerations in mind, you can ensure a safer, more comfortable trip while enjoying all the natural beauty and adventure Costa Rica has to offer.

Do's and Don'ts While in Costa Rica

Costa Rica is known for its "Pura Vida" lifestyle, which embodies a laid-back, friendly attitude and a deep respect for nature. As a visitor, understanding how to interact with the culture and environment respectfully will enhance your experience. Here are some Do's and Don'ts for your trip:

- **Do** embrace the "Pura Vida" mindset by adopting a positive, relaxed attitude and greeting people with "Pura Vida."

- **Don't** engage in aggressive bargaining, as Costa Ricans typically prefer a more respectful and gentle approach to negotiating prices.

- **Do** dress modestly and respectfully, especially in rural areas, religious sites, and public spaces.

- **Don't** swim in dangerous waters or ignore posted warnings, particularly regarding strong rip currents on the Pacific coast.

- **Do** support eco-friendly tourism by choosing tours, accommodations, and activities that prioritize sustainability and conservation.

- **Don't** rush interactions—Costa Ricans value a slower, relaxed pace, so be patient and allow time for things to unfold.

- **Do** be friendly and greet locals with a warm "¡Hola!" or "Buenos días!", as Costa Ricans are known for their hospitality.

- **Don't** assume that everyone speaks English, especially in rural areas. Make an effort to speak a little Spanish or use translation apps when needed.

TOURIST TAXATION

TOURIST TAXATION

Overview

Tourism plays a crucial role in Costa Rica's broader economic framework as **one of the largest contributors to its GDP**. The country is known for its rich biodiversity, eco-tourism opportunities, and natural beauty, attracting millions of international visitors each year. Tourism supports a wide range of industries, from hospitality and transportation to agriculture and services, providing jobs for thousands of locals. The influx of tourists generates significant foreign exchange, which is vital for the country's economy, helping to fund various public projects, social programs, and national development initiatives. Eco-tourism, in particular, has become a cornerstone of Costa Rica's strategy to balance environmental preservation with economic growth.

Tourists are required to pay **taxes** in Costa Rica because tourism is considered a **key revenue source for the country**. These taxes, like the *impuesto de salida* (exit tax) and *impuesto de ventas* (sales tax), help ensure that tourists contribute to the cost of maintaining public services and infrastructure that they use during their stay. Since tourism significantly impacts local economies—especially in popular tourist destinations— it's important that tourists share in the financial responsibilities of sustaining the country's resources, services, and national development.

Tourist taxes in Costa Rica directly contribute to the **funding of public services and infrastructure**, which are essential for both locals and visitors. The funds generated from taxes are used to improve and maintain infrastructure such as roads, airports, parks, and public transportation systems. Additionally, these taxes support healthcare, education, environmental conservation efforts, and public safety—services that benefit both residents and tourists. As Costa Rica's economy relies heavily on tourism, these taxes help maintain the quality of the visitor experience while also supporting sustainable development in the country.

Tourist Taxes in Costa Rica

When traveling to Costa Rica, tourists encounter several types of taxes that help fund the country's infrastructure and public services. The most common of these is the **Exit Tax** or *Impuesto de Salida*. This tax is typically included in the price of your international flight ticket, so you won't have to worry about paying it separately. However, if it's not included, you can pay it directly at the airport before departure, usually around **US$29**.

In addition, Costa Rica introduced a **Value Added Tax** (VAT), a **13% sales tax** applied to most goods and services, including hotel stays, tours, meals, and souvenirs. This tax is automatically added to your bill when you make a purchase or use a service, so tourists don't have to think about calculating it—it's simply included in the price.

For those staying in hotels, there's also a **Tourism Development Tax**, which supports the growth and maintenance of Costa Rica's tourism infrastructure. This small fee, typically around **US$1–3** per night, is usually added to your accommodation bill, so you won't need to pay it separately.

If you're traveling by air, be aware of **airport service fees**, which are often bundled with your flight ticket. These fees help maintain the airports and services tourists rely on. While you may not always notice them, they contribute to the overall cost of your travel experience.

Lastly, if you plan on visiting Costa Rica's stunning national parks, you'll encounter **national park entry fees**, which are an essential part of preserving the country's natural beauty. These fees, ranging from **US$10–15**, are paid at the park entrance and help fund conservation efforts, ensuring that these pristine environments remain protected for future generations.

 **Law of the Land Hypothetical**

HYPOTHETICAL: *Emma, a tourist in Costa Rica, noticed her hotel correctly charged the Tourism Development Tax and that her airline ticket included the Exit Tax. However, she realized that the 13% VAT sales tax wasn't added to the price of her guided tour to Manuel Antonio National Park. She wonders if the tour operator is required to charge her VAT and if she can get a refund for the oversight. Is the tour operator required by law to charge Emma the 13% VAT on the tour, and can she request a refund if they didn't?*

ANSWER: Yes, *under Costa Rican law, the VAT is mandatory on most goods and services, including tours. The tour operator is required to add the 13% tax to the tour price. If they failed to do so, Emma is entitled to request a refund or adjustment. She can ask the tour operator for the correction, and if needed, report the issue to Costa Rica's Dirección General de Tributación (tax authority). The Tourism Development Tax charged by the hotel is also correct and in line with regulations.*

LONG-TERM STAYS

CHAPTER 23

LONG-TERM STAYS

Overview

Many people choose to stay long-term in Costa Rica for its stunning natural beauty, affordable cost of living, and vibrant cultural scene. The country's pristine beaches, lush rainforests, and towering volcanoes make it a haven for nature lovers, while its low cost of living—especially in less touristy regions—attracts retirees, digital nomads, and expats alike. Costa Rica's friendly locals, emphasis on environmental conservation, and laid-back "pura vida" lifestyle further enhance its appeal. Moreover, Costa Rica offers a variety of tax incentives for retirees, making it an even more attractive destination for those seeking to relocate.

An English-speaking population and established expat communities in places like **San José**, **Escazú**, and **Nosara** provide newcomers with a comfortable environment in which to settle. High-quality healthcare, eco-friendly living options, and easy access to the U.S. and Canada contribute to Costa Rica's growing reputation as a top destination for long-term living. While safety can be a concern in certain urban areas, many of the most popular expat regions are secure, offering a peaceful and safe living environment.

Best Regions and Cities for Long-Term Living in Costa Rica

Costa Rica offers a diverse range of living options, with each region catering to different lifestyles. **San José**, the capital, is ideal for those

seeking modern amenities, cultural experiences, and career opportunities, though it can be a bit fast-paced compared to other areas. Expats
looking for a balance of nature and urban convenience may find **Escazú**
or **Santa Ana** appealing, as they offer proximity to San José's amenities
without the hustle and bustle.

For a quieter and more laid-back lifestyle, regions like **Nosara**,
Tamarindo, and **Dominical** offer a perfect combination of natural
beauty and slower-paced living. These coastal areas are popular with retirees and remote workers due to their stunning beaches, good internet
connectivity, and vibrant expat communities.

If you're a nature lover, **La Fortuna** near Arenal Volcano offers an incredible backdrop of volcanic landscapes, hot springs, and abundant
wildlife, while **Monteverde** is the ideal choice for those wanting to live
among the clouds in the heart of the cloud forest.

The **Caribbean Coast**, especially areas like **Puerto Viejo** and **Cahuita**,
offer a unique vibe, with Afro-Caribbean culture, beautiful beaches, and
a laid-back atmosphere. **Quepos** and **Manuel Antonio** are well-known
for their proximity to a national park and beautiful beaches, making
them great for those who want to be close to nature but still enjoy modern comforts.

Living Costs in Costa Rica[42]

The cost of living in Costa Rica is generally much lower than in the
United States or many Western countries, making it an affordable destination for long-term residents. Most daily expenses, from housing to
food, are more budget-friendly, though imported goods may still carry
a premium price.

- **Housing:** Rent is one of the biggest savings for expats in Costa Rica.
  A one-bedroom apartment in a major city like San José typically
  costs around **US$500–$800** per month, while in rural areas, it can

---

42 https://www.expatistan.com/cost-of-living/country/costa-rica

drop to **US$300–$500**. Larger homes or luxury rentals can also be more affordable compared to the U.S.

▪ **Utilities:** Utilities, including electricity, water, and internet, cost around **US$150** per month on average, though this can vary depending on the location and lifestyle.

▪ **Food and Dining:** Groceries are quite affordable in Costa Rica, with a monthly grocery bill averaging about **US$300** per person. Dining out is also much cheaper, with a meal at a mid-range restaurant costing around **US$10–$15**.

▪ **Transportation:** Public transportation is very affordable in Costa Rica, with bus fares averaging around **US$0.75**. Taxis and private rides are also widely available, with a short ride typically costing about **US$5–$10**. Renting a car for a month typically costs around **US$500–$700**.

▪ **Healthcare:** Healthcare in Costa Rica is both affordable and of high quality. A doctor's visit usually costs around **US$50–$75**, compared to **US$150–$300** in the U.S. Costa Rica's public healthcare system, **Caja Costarricense de Seguro Social** (CCSS), is available to all residents and expats, with a monthly contribution based on income. Private healthcare is also available and is often preferred by expats for faster service.

Housing Options for Long-Term Stays

Costa Rica offers a wide variety of **rental options**, catering to all preferences and budgets. You can find everything from modern apartments in the city to rustic homes in the countryside. Popular areas like Escazú, Tamarindo, and Nosara have numerous rental properties, ranging from cozy studios to luxury villas. Rental options in San José provide easy access to city amenities, while more rural locations offer tranquility and stunning views.

For those looking for a quieter and more isolated environment, areas like La Fortuna, Monteverde, and Puerto Viejo provide affordable cottages, cabins, or homes tucked away in nature. Many rental properties come fully furnished and include internet, making them ideal for long-term stays. Gated communities are also common in popular expat regions, offering additional security and amenities like swimming pools and gyms.

Transportation Options

Costa Rica offers various transportation options, depending on where you live and your personal preferences.

- **Public Transportation:** The bus system is one of the most affordable ways to get around Costa Rica, with extensive routes connecting even rural areas. However, buses can be slow and less reliable than other forms of transport.

- **Taxis and Ride-Sharing:** Taxis are widely available, especially in urban areas. Prices are relatively affordable, but it's best to ensure the driver uses the meter. Ride-sharing apps like **Uber** also operate in some areas, offering a convenient alternative.

- **Car Rentals:** Renting a car is an excellent option for those wishing to explore the country at their own pace. While driving in Costa Rica can be a bit challenging due to winding roads and varying road conditions, car rentals are affordable, and many visitors find it convenient to drive around.

- **Biking:** In areas like Tamarindo, Nosara, and Escazú, biking is a popular way to get around, especially with the temperate climate and well-maintained roads.

Healthcare Options for Long-Term Visitors

Costa Rica is known for its high-quality healthcare system, which is both affordable and accessible. Expats can choose between public and private healthcare.

- **Public Healthcare:** The Caja Costarricense de Seguro Social (CCSS) offers comprehensive public healthcare for all residents, including expatriates. This system provides low-cost healthcare but may involve longer waiting times for certain services.

- **Private Healthcare:** Costa Rica also has an excellent private healthcare system, with hospitals and clinics offering a wide range of services. Popular private healthcare providers include CIMA and **Clinica Biblica** in San José. Private care is often preferred by expats for shorter wait times and personalized services, though it is more expensive than public healthcare.

- **Health Insurance:** While public healthcare is available to expatriates, many choose to invest in private international health insurance plans to cover additional services or avoid long waiting times. Costa Rica's medical services are generally much more affordable than in North America or Europe.

Language Considerations

Spanish is the official language of Costa Rica, and while English is widely spoken, especially in touristy areas and expat communities, learning some basic Spanish can greatly enhance your experience. Many Costa Ricans are friendly and appreciative when visitors make an effort to speak the local language, even if it's just a few phrases.

Costa Rican Spanish is relatively clear and straightforward, making it easier for beginners to learn. While it's not necessary to speak fluent Spanish for day-to-day living, having a basic understanding can help you navigate daily interactions, such as shopping, transportation, and dealing with local authorities.

In tourist areas and expat communities, English is commonly spoken, and most public services (e.g., healthcare, banking, education) are available in both Spanish and English. However, learning Spanish can deepen your connection with locals and enrich your cultural experience.

Overall, Costa Rica is a welcoming and affordable destination with a high quality of life, making it an ideal choice for long-term living. Whether you're seeking adventure, peace, or a new chapter in your life, this "pura vida" paradise has something for everyone.

Long-Term Visas[43]

Costa Rica offers several long-term visa options:

- **Pensionado Visa:** For retirees with a guaranteed income of at least US$1,000/month. Includes benefits like tax exemptions on personal items and the ability to work. After 3 years, you can apply for permanent residency.

- **Rentista Visa:** For those with a stable income (e.g., US$2,500/month) or a US$60,000 deposit. After 3 years, you can apply for permanent residency.

- **Inversionista Visa:** For those investing at least US$200,000 in Costa Rica (e.g., real estate or business). Permanent residency after 2 years.

- **Work Visa:** For those with a Costa Rican job offer, sponsored by an employer. Temporary residency for 1-2 years, with family included.

- **Student Visa:** For enrolled students in Costa Rican institutions. Limited work rights, and generally temporary.

- **Digital Nomad Visa:** For remote workers with a US$3,000/month income (or US$4,000 for families). Valid for 1 year, extendable. Exempt from taxes on foreign income.

- **Permanent Residency:** Available after 3 years of temporary residency (e.g., *Rentista*, *Pensionado*, or *Inversionista*). Allows indefinite stay and work.

- **Refugee/Humanitarian Visas:** For individuals fleeing persecution, typically leading to permanent residency after some time.

The process of obtaining a long-term visa in Costa Rica begins with choosing the right visa based on your situation—whether it's for retirement, income, investment, or remote work. Once you've chosen the appropriate visa, you'll need to gather **required documents** like a valid passport, proof of income, police clearance, medical certificates, and any additional paperwork, such as investment records or family documents if you're including dependents.

---

43 https://goldenharbors.com/articles/costa-rica-residency

After assembling everything, you'll **submit your application** to Costa Rica's Immigration Department, either in person or online. The approval process can take anywhere from a few weeks to a few months, and during this time, immigration may ask for additional information. Upon approval, you'll receive **temporary residency**, allowing you to live in Costa Rica for 1 to 3 years, depending on the visa type. During this period, you may also be able to work or manage a business, depending on your visa. After meeting the required time frame, usually 2 to 3 years, you can apply for permanent residency. If you've followed the visa conditions, this step is typically straightforward, granting you the ability to stay and work in Costa Rica indefinitely.

Throughout the process, it's wise to work with an **immigration lawyer** or consultant to ensure that your application is complete and that you meet all legal requirements. With careful preparation, you'll be well on your way to living in Costa Rica long-term.

 **General Questions**

1. *If I want to stay in Costa Rica for long-term and work, should I apply for a work permit before arriving in Costa Rica?*
   No. You don't need to apply for a work permit before arriving in Costa Rica. To work legally, you'll need a job offer from a Costa Rican employer who will sponsor your visa. Once you arrive, your employer will submit the necessary paperwork to secure your work visa, allowing you to live and work in Costa Rica legally.

2. *I am American. Can I retire to Costa Rica?* **Yes.** As an American, you can retire to Costa Rica. The Pensionado Visa allows retirees to live in Costa Rica if they have a guaranteed monthly income of at least US$1,000 (from a pension or Social Security). This visa grants residency, and after three years, you can apply for permanent residency.

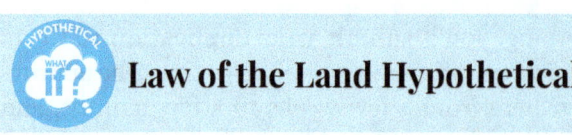

Law of the Land Hypothetical

HYPOTHETICAL: *John, a 35-year-old digital marketer from New York, has been working remotely for a company based in the U.S. for the past two years. He's fallen in love with Costa Rica after visiting on vacation and wants to move there long-term. John is considering applying for the Digital Nomad Visa, but he's unsure if he meets the income requirements and whether he needs to prove his employment with a specific company. Additionally, he wonders if he can bring his girlfriend along, and whether she would need to apply for a separate visa. Does John qualify for the Digital Nomad Visa with a monthly income of US$3,500? Can he bring his girlfriend, and does she need to apply for her own visa?*

ANSWER: *John qualifies for the Digital Nomad Visa because his monthly income of US$3,500 meets the minimum requirement of US$3,000 for single applicants, or US$4,000 for applicants with dependents. Since he works remotely for a U.S.-based company and is not seeking employment in Costa Rica, this visa is the ideal option for him. His girlfriend can also join him in Costa Rica, but she will need to apply for her own dependent visa under the same application. While John's Digital Nomad Visa covers his residency, his girlfriend will be considered a dependent and must provide proof of their relationship, as well as meet the other documentation requirements (such as a valid passport and police clearance). The Digital Nomad Visa is valid for one year and can be renewed for an additional year. John and his girlfriend will both enjoy the benefits of being residents, such as tax exemptions on income earned outside Costa Rica and the ability to live and work remotely.*

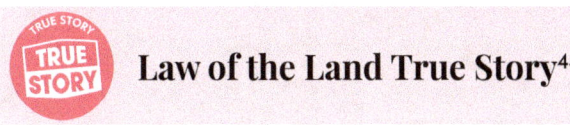

Law of the Land True Story[44]

Starting on April 20, 2018, Costa Rica began charging a US$100 per month fee for foreign visitors who overstay their visas. This new penalty applies to all overstays that have occurred since March 1, 2010, when the General Law of Immigration took effect. The Costa Rican Immigration Administration announced that the fee would be charged upon departure from the country.

If the overstayer fails to pay the penalty, they will face a reentry ban to Costa Rica for a period equal to three times the duration of their overstay. This penalty is based on Article 33 of the Immigration Law, which stipulates that foreigners must leave the country when their authorized stay expires, unless they request an extension or category change.

Individuals can check the amount they owe on the Immigration website and make the payment at Banco de Costa Rica branches, certain Post Office locations, or other authorized points across the country. For more information or questions about the fee, individuals can contact Costa Rican Immigration or the Banco de Costa Rica customer service.

---

44 https://ticotimes.net/2018/03/20/
  immigration-charges-100-per-month-for-overstaying-visa-in-costa-rica

 **Takeaways**

- Known for its natural beauty and affordable cost of living, Costa Rica attracts retirees, digital nomads, and expats with its beaches, rainforests, and relaxed "pura vida" lifestyle.

- Popular areas for expats include San José for urban living, Escazú for nature and convenience, and coastal spots like Nosara and Tamarindo for a laid-back lifestyle.

- Costa Rica offers various long-term visas, such as the Pensionado Visa for retirees and the Digital Nomad Visa for remote workers. Most visas lead to permanent residency after 2-3 years.

- Costa Rica's healthcare system is both high-quality and affordable, with many expats opting for private care.

- Costa Rica has well-established expat communities in places like Escazú and Nosara, making it easy for newcomers to settle and find support.

CIVIL LITIGATION

CHAPTER 24

CIVIL LITIGATION

Overview

Civil litigation provides a mechanism for resolving disputes, ensuring that travelers have a way to seek justice if legal issues arise while visiting another country. It helps them understand their rights and obligations under local laws, which may differ from those in their home country. The civil litigation system offers a formal process for addressing conflicts, such as contract disputes or personal injury claims, and can deter unfair practices by encouraging businesses to comply with legal standards. It also allows individuals to seek financial recourse for damages or losses and helps protect them from potential exploitation by local entities. Overall, understanding civil litigation enhances a visitor's experience and safety while traveling.

Personal Injury Claims and Compensation Law

Personal injury claims in Costa Rica are predicated on several grounds, including negligence, intentional acts, and strict liability. **Negligence** is perhaps the most common basis for these claims, where a party fails to exercise reasonable care, resulting in harm to another individual. For example, in a slip and fall case, a property owner's failure to maintain safe premises could establish negligence. Additionally, **intentional acts**, such as assault, can also provide grounds for a personal injury claim. Here, the victim may seek damages based on the deliberate harm caused by the perpetrator Lastly, **strict liability** cases may involve situations, such as defective products, where a claimant does not need to prove fault but only the occurrence of harm due to the product. To establish grounds for a claim, the injured party must demonstrate that their injury was caused by the fault (negligence, recklessness, or intentional wrongdoing) of another party.[45]

To file a personal injury claim, the injured person should first seek medical attention to **document the injury** and ensure proper treatment. If necessary, the incident should be reported to the authorities, such as in the case of a car accident. This official report can play a crucial role as evidence.

Next, it's important to **consult with a lawyer** who specializes in personal injury law. The lawyer will help navigate the legal process and gather essential evidence, such as medical records, police reports, photographs, and witness testimonies. The claim can be pursued either through direct negotiations with the responsible party's insurance company or through the court system if a settlement cannot be reached. While many cases are settled outside of court, unresolved claims may proceed to trial for further adjudication.[46]

How Are Damages Calculated

The calculation of damages in personal injury claims in Costa Rica adheres to particular legal standards that address various forms of compensation. Damages in personal injury claims are typically divided into two categories:

1. **Compensatory Damages:** These are intended to compensate the victim for the actual harm they suffered. They include:

   - **Medical expenses:** Past and future medical costs related to the injury.

---

45 https://pirielegal.com/civil-law-in-costa-rica

46 https://ticotimes.net/2024/12/29/a-guide-to-litigation-in-costa-rica

- **Lost wages:** If the injury caused the individual to miss work, compensation for lost earnings is included.

- **Pain and suffering:** Compensation for physical and emotional distress.

- **Loss of quality of life:** If the injury results in permanent disability or diminished capacity to enjoy life.

2. **Punitive Damages:** These are awarded to punish the responsible party and deter similar conduct in the future. However, punitive damages are less common in Costa Rica compared to other countries like the United States.

Damages are usually calculated based on the evidence provided, including medical records, expert testimony, and documentation of any financial losses incurred due to the injury.[47]

Role of Insurance

Insurance is a crucial component of personal injury claims in Costa Rica. Depending on the nature of the accident, various insurance policies may come into play:

- **Automobile insurance:** In traffic accidents, both the victim and the responsible party may have insurance policies. Costa Rica requires liability insurance for all vehicles, which covers damages to others in the event of an accident. You can file a claim through your own insurance or that of the responsible driver.

- **Worker's compensation insurance:** In cases of workplace injury, employers in Costa Rica are required by law to provide insurance coverage for workplace injuries. This system is handled through the Caja Costarricense de Seguro Social (CCSS), which is Costa Rica's social security system. You may be entitled to benefits for medical treatment and partial disability.

---

47 https://costaricalaw.com/costa-rica-legal-topics/litigation-in-costa-rica/ civil-liability-for-slip-and-fall-accidents-in-costa-rica-comparing-the- united-states-and-costa-rica-systems/

- **Private health insurance:** If you have private health insurance, it may cover medical expenses, but the amount you're reimbursed may depend on your policy terms.

You'll need to work with insurance adjusters to determine the amount of compensation you can receive, and sometimes the insurer will offer a settlement before a formal lawsuit is filed.[48]

Related Legal Fee

Legal fees in personal injury cases in Costa Rica can **vary significantly** based on several factors, including the complexity of the case and the attorney's experience. Most personal injury lawyers operate on a **contingency fee** basis, meaning they receive a percentage of the settlement or award upon winning the case, typically ranging from 30 to 40 percent. Initial consultations are frequently offered at no cost, allowing potential claimants to assess their options without financial risk. However, if a case moves forward to litigation, various court fees, filing fees, and potential expert witness costs may arise, which claimants should be prepared for when planning to pursue legal action.

How to File a Civil Claim[49]

Filing a civil claim in Costa Rica involves a clear process governed by the country's legal system. To begin, you must **determine the type of civil claim** you wish to pursue, which can range from issues related to contracts, property disputes, family matters, or torts, among others. Once you've identified the type of claim, the next step is to **ensure you meet the necessary requirements**, which generally include having standing in the case (meaning you must have a legal interest in the matter), sufficient evidence to support your claim, and the proper legal capacity to file.

---

48 https://www.bautistaleroy.com/
understanding-injury-lawsuits-against-tourism-companies

49 https://pirielegal.com/litigation-lawsuit-costa-rica

The claim should be **supported by specific documents**, including identification (such as your national ID card or passport), proof of ownership or contractual agreements, and any correspondence or evidence pertinent to the case, such as invoices, photographs, or witness statements. Additionally, you'll need to **prepare a formal written complaint** outlining the facts, the legal basis for your claim, and the relief you seek.

The claim is then **filed at the appropriate court**, depending on the nature and value of the dispute. For lower-value claims, this will typically be a **Civil Court**, while larger or more complex claims might require filing in a higher court such as the **Tribunal de Justicia**. Claims can also be filed in **specialized courts** depending on the issue at hand, such as family or labor courts.

It's important to ensure **all documents are translated into Spanish** if they are in another language, and that any **applicable fees are paid.** After the claim is filed, the court will assign a date for the hearing, and the process will proceed from there, potentially involving mediation or further legal actions based on the specifics of the case.

Service of Documents[50]

In Costa Rica, the service of documents is governed by the Civil Procedure Code, which outlines the formal procedures to ensure that parties involved in a legal dispute are properly notified. The legal framework ensures that service of process is conducted in a fair and transparent manner, enabling parties to be informed of lawsuits, hearings, or other significant legal actions.

The primary methods of service in Costa Rica include **personal service**, where the document is handed directly to the individual or their representative; **postal service**, through certified mail or an equivalent official service; and in some cases, **service by publication** in newspapers for individuals whose whereabouts are unknown. Depending on the case,

---

50 https://undisputedlegal.com/code-of-civil-procedure-of-costa-rica/

service can also be executed **through judicial officers or bailiffs** who carry out the delivery of legal documents.

The responsibility for serving documents generally falls on the party initiating the lawsuit, typically through a legal representative or a process server. The procedure begins when the documents are presented to the relevant authorities, who then ensure the correct service method is used. If the recipient cannot be found at their residence, the authorities may attempt to serve the documents at an alternate location, such as their workplace, or via other authorized methods. The service process typically involves an attempt to deliver the documents directly, and if that fails, further attempts or alternatives are pursued according to the law. Once service is completed, **proof of service** must be documented by the server, often through a signed acknowledgment of receipt by the recipient or a formal report detailing the methods and attempts made to serve the documents.

If service is unsuccessful after multiple attempts, the court may authorize other measures, such as service by publication. The proof of service becomes part of the case file, and the court uses this documentation to confirm that due process has been followed.

Statute of Limitations

In Costa Rica, the statute of limitations for civil suits **varies depending on the type of claim** being filed. Generally, the Civil Code stipulates different periods for different types of claims, with time limits ranging from one to ten years. For example, **personal injury claims** must be filed within **three years**, while **contract disputes** typically have a limitation period of **five years**. Claims related to **real property** (such as ownership disputes) are generally subject to a limitation period of **ten years**. However, shorter periods may apply in specific instances, such as **debt claims**, which often require action within **three years**.

Several factors can affect the length of the statute of limitations. These can include the nature of the claim, whether the claim involves individuals or corporations, or the discovery of a latent injury or fraud, which may extend the period in certain cases. The statute of limitations may also be **suspended or interrupted** if certain events occur, such as the defendant's **absence from the country** or if the claimant is a **minor** or **mentally incapacitated**.

If a civil suit is filed after the statute of limitations has expired, the court will typically **dismiss the case**, and the claim will not be heard on its merits. However, there are exceptions where the statute of limitations can be **extended** or tolled, such as when the defendant has actively concealed their actions (**fraudulent concealment**), or if the claimant was **unaware** of the damage due to circumstances beyond their control. These exceptions are considered on a case-by-case basis, and the burden of proof rests with the claimant to demonstrate the reason for the delay.[51]

 ## Getting Married in Costa Rica[52]

Getting married in Costa Rica involves a straightforward legal process, but there are specific requirements and documents necessary to ensure the marriage is valid. To marry in Costa Rica, couples must meet the legal age requirement, which is **18 years old** for both parties. If either party is **under 18**, they must obtain **court approval** in addition to **parental consent**.

Foreign nationals can marry in Costa Rica without residency requirements, but they must present certain documents to apply for a marriage license. These documents typically include **valid passports** (or another form of government-issued identification), **birth certificates**, and proof that neither party is currently married, which may be established through an **affidavit stating marital status**. In some cases,

---

51   https://pirielegal.com/civil-law-in-costa-rica

52   https://www.elopeincostarica.com/eloping_in_costa_rica/
     costa-rica-marriage-laws/)

certified copies of divorce decrees or death certificates (if applicable) will also be required.

The process for obtaining a **marriage license** in Costa Rica generally begins at the **Civil Registry Office**. Both parties must be present in person to submit their application. Once the necessary documents are submitted and verified, the couple can obtain a marriage license, which permits them to marry. There is no formal waiting period in Costa Rica, and the process is typically quick, often taking just a few hours to a day depending on the office and any document verification requirements. For foreign nationals, additional steps such as the **apostille** or legalization of foreign documents may be needed, depending on the country of origin of the documents.

The application process itself is relatively fast, and most marriages are legally valid once the ceremony has taken place, whether conducted in a religious or civil context. After the marriage, the couple receives a **marriage certificate**, which can be used for legal purposes such as changing names or applying for residency. Although there are no residency requirements for foreign nationals, it is important that **documents** in a foreign language are **translated into Spanish** by a certified translator before submission to the authorities.

After the ceremony, the officiant is responsible for registering the marriage with the **Costa Rican Civil Registry**, and it typically takes several weeks for the official marriage certificate to be processed and sent. Couples should ensure that the marriage certificate is translated and **authenticated through their embassy** if they intend to use it abroad. Marriages conducted in Costa Rica are **legally recognized internationally**, including in countries like the United States and Canada, although couples should verify their home country's requirements for registering foreign marriages to avoid complications.

In Costa Rica, a **civil ceremony** is typically officiated by a notary or lawyer, and couples have the flexibility to choose the location of their ceremony, which can take place in various scenic settings. **Religious ceremonies**, however, are held in Catholic churches and must adhere to specific religious guidelines, such as presenting a certificate of single status and possibly attending premarital counseling.

The **fees** for getting married in Costa Rica can vary, with officiant fees ranging from US$600 to $1,000, which may include both the ceremony and legal paperwork, while additional costs can arise from venue rentals, catering, and other services.[53]

 ## Law of the Land Hypothetical

HYPOTHETICAL: *Maria, a U.S. citizen, is vacationing in Costa Rica and has a slip-and-fall accident at a hotel. She sustains a serious injury and incurs significant medical bills. After receiving treatment, Maria decides to file a personal injury claim against the hotel, seeking compensation for her medical expenses and lost wages. What are Maria's rights and the steps she must take to file her personal injury claim in Costa Rica, and what factors will affect the amount of compensation she may receive?*

ANSWER: *Maria, a U.S. citizen, can file a personal injury claim in Costa Rica if she can prove the hotel's negligence caused her injury. To start, she should seek medical treatment and gather documents like medical records and accident reports. Consulting with a local attorney specializing in personal injury is essential, as they will help file a formal complaint outlining the facts, legal basis, and compensation sought. She can claim compensatory damages for medical expenses, lost wages, and pain and suffering, and potentially punitive damages. The amount of compensation will depend on the severity of her injury and the hotel's role in the accident. The statute of limitations for personal injury claims in Costa Rica is three years, so Maria must file within that time. If the hotel has insurance, she may settle the case out of court; otherwise, the case may proceed to trial.*

---

53 https://www.destinationweddingdirec-
    tory.co/south-america-wedding-guides/
    getting-married-in-costa-rica-costa-rican-wedding-guide

CHAPTER 25
OTHER THINGS TO KNOW

241

OTHER THINGS TO KNOW

Tourists and Street Hustling

Street hustling in Costa Rica, particularly in tourist areas, involves individuals using aggressive or deceptive tactics to sell goods or services to visitors. Common behaviors include persistent approaches by vendors or individuals offering **unsolicited services**, such as guides, photographers, or even "free" samples of products. Street hustlers may also use **manipulation**, like pretending to befriend tourists or offering deals that seem too good to be true, only to later demand more money than initially agreed.

Goods commonly offered by street hustlers include handmade crafts, jewelry, t-shirts, sunglasses, and local artwork. **Services** might include guided tours, transportation, or street performances. These offers are often aimed at tourists who may be unfamiliar with local prices and customs. In popular tourist destinations like **San José, Jaco Beach, Manuel Antonio**, and **Puerto Viejo**, street hustling is more prevalent, especially in areas with heavy foot traffic or near tourist hotspots like beaches, markets, and cultural sites.

Some common scams tourists should watch out for include **overpriced souvenirs**, where a vendor inflates prices significantly for foreigners, or **"fake" tour guides** who offer tours but lack proper credentials. Another scam involves **"complimentary" services** like a free drink or photo, followed by an unexpectedly high charge. Tourists may also encounter **pickpocketing** or individuals offering fake tickets for attractions.

Local authorities, along with tourism organizations, do address street hustling through increased **patrols** in high-traffic areas and **awareness campaigns** for tourists. In some cases, businesses and local tourism boards collaborate to educate visitors about scams and provide guidance on how to avoid falling victim to street hustlers. However, while street hustling is illegal, enforcement can sometimes be inconsistent, and it's generally up to tourists to be cautious and informed.

Safety Concerns and Practical Tips

Interacting with street hustlers in Costa Rica can pose several safety concerns, especially in high-traffic tourist areas. **Aggressive behavior** from hustlers is a common issue, as they may pressure tourists into buying overpriced goods or accepting unwanted services. In some cases, hustlers may try to deceive visitors into paying for products that are either of poor quality or non-existent. There are also risks of **pickpocketing** and scams, where tourists might be distracted while others steal personal belongings.

To protect themselves, tourists should take several **precautions**. First, they should be cautious about engaging with hustlers offering unsolicited goods or services, particularly in crowded or unfamiliar areas. It's advisable to **avoid showing large amounts of cash** or valuable items like cameras or jewelry while walking in busy tourist spots. Tourists can also **set firm boundaries** with street hustlers—politely but firmly declining offers without getting into prolonged conversations. If the interaction becomes uncomfortable, walking away quickly is recommended. Additionally, tourists should **always stay aware of their surroundings** and avoid distractions, such as using their phone while on the street.

Local customs and behaviors can help tourists navigate interactions safely. In Costa Rica, **politeness** is key, but tourists should not feel obligated to engage in prolonged conversations if they don't want to. A simple **"no, gracias"** (no, thank you) is usually enough to politely decline any offers. It's also important to remember that in Costa Rican culture, direct refusals are generally respected, and it's perfectly acceptable to avoid further discussion with hustlers.

If tourists experience harassment or fall victim to a scam, they can report the incident to local authorities or tourism offices. Many popular tourist areas have **tourism police,** who can assist in cases of harassment or fraud. Tourists can also contact the **Costa Rican Tourism Institute** (ICT), which provides information and support for visitors facing such issues. Additionally, some cities and regions have **tourism help desks** at popular hotels, airports, and local tourist information centers where visitors can file complaints and receive advice on how to avoid future incidents.

 ## In the Event of Death

If someone traveling with you dies in Costa Rica, the situation can be overwhelming, but there are important steps to take to manage the process legally and respectfully.

First, **contact the local authorities** immediately, either the Costa Rican police or an ambulance service, to report the death. If the death occurs in a hospital, they will handle the initial formalities. The police will investigate the cause of death, especially if it is unexpected or suspicious, and may require a death certificate issued by a Costa Rican doctor. In the event of an unnatural death (e.g., an accident), a local forensic doctor may also be involved.

Next, reach out to your **embassy or consulate.** They can assist with the process, such as coordinating the repatriation of the body, helping to arrange funeral services, and providing guidance on the necessary paperwork. The embassy can also inform family members back home and advise them on the next steps. The U.S. embassy, for instance, can also provide a list of funeral homes and local services in Costa Rica that specialize in dealing with repatriation.

Handling the deceased's remains involves several important steps. If you wish to have the body returned home, it is necessary to **contact a funeral home** in Costa Rica, as they will guide you through embalming and preparation for transportation. The Ministry of Health must issue a **funeral export certificate**, which is required to transport the body internationally. Additionally, the body must be properly embalmed, and a consular mortuary certificate will be issued by the embassy or consulate.

For families planning to bring the body home, they should be prepared for various **costs** involved in the repatriation process, including **embalming, caskets, transportation**, and the various **legal fees** for required certificates. Depending on the country of destination, the embassy or consulate can assist in ensuring that all necessary paperwork is in order for the body's arrival. It's also crucial to know that certain health requirements may apply before transporting human remains internationally.[54]

Experiencing Financial Hardship

Tourists in Costa Rica may face financial hardship due to a variety of reasons. Some common causes include **unexpected medical emergencies, theft** or **loss of credit cards**, or **overspending** due to unfamiliarity with local prices. Additionally, tourists might not realize the cost of certain activities, accommodations, or transportation, which can quickly add up. **ATMs or card payment issues**, such as international transaction fees or being unable to access funds, may also contribute to financial challenges.

If tourists run out of money or find themselves in financial distress, they should first **contact** their **bank or credit card company** to inquire

---

54   http://costarica-information.com/about-costa-rica/economy/economic-sectors-industries/real-estate/real-estate-general/living-in-costa-rica/medical/death-in-costa-rica#

about **emergency cash transfers** or **temporarily increasing their credit limit**. They can also use **money transfer services** like Western Union or MoneyGram to receive funds from family or friends. In emergencies, **local embassies** or **consulates** may assist by providing a list of resources or helping to arrange a temporary loan or travel funds, although they generally do not provide direct financial assistance. It's also advisable to keep emergency contact numbers handy for insurance providers or services that can help with urgent needs.

Costa Rica has several support systems for travelers facing financial hardship. **Tourism police** in major tourist areas can offer advice and help connect travelers to local services, including financial institutions that may assist with emergency fund transfers. Many **local banks** accept international cards and offer currency exchange services. Additionally, some **travel insurance policies** can help cover unexpected costs like medical emergencies or theft. Services like Western Union and PayPal also allow for quick transfers from abroad.

Understanding the local currency, the Costa Rican colón (CRC), is essential for managing expenses. While U.S. dollars are accepted in many tourist areas, the exchange rate may not be in your favor, and you may receive change in colones. It's important to check the exchange rate before exchanging money to ensure you're getting a fair deal. **Cash withdrawals from ATMs** may incur **international fees**, so it's best to limit these withdrawals to avoid excessive charges. Restaurants, transportation, and activities in touristy areas tend to be more expensive, so visiting local markets and eateries can help save money.

To avoid financial strain, **budgeting** is key. Tourists should plan and track their daily expenses, including accommodation, food, and activities. **Public transportation** is a cost-effective option, and tourists can opt for **self-guided tours** rather than expensive guided ones. Setting aside an **emergency fund** and ensuring a **backup payment method** (e.g., an extra credit card) is available can help avoid sudden financial challenges. By being proactive with budgeting and understanding local costs, tourists can better manage their finances and minimize the risk of hardship while traveling in Costa Rica.

QUICK REFERENCE GUIDE

- Quick Chapter References to Important Topics

QUICK REFERENCE GUIDE

Crime in Costa Rica

Are there particular areas I should avoid as a tourist?

While Costa Rica is generally safe for tourists, it's advisable to exercise caution in areas like San José's downtown and neighborhoods like La Carpio and Pavas, as they have higher crime rates. Similarly, Limón and parts of the Pacific coast (e.g., Jacó and Quepos) are known for petty theft and occasional muggings. Always stay aware of your surroundings, avoid walking alone at night, and secure valuables to minimize risks. *For more details, see Chapter 3.*

Drug Offenses

Is the possession of marijuana legal?

No. The possession of marijuana is not fully legal in Costa Rica, though small amounts for personal use are decriminalized.

Is the possession of cocaine legal?

No. The possession of cocaine is illegal in Costa Rica, and penalties for possession are severe. *For more details, see Chapter 4.*

Alcohol-Related Offenses

What is the legal drinking age?

> The legal drinking age in Costa Rica is **18 years old.**

What is the legal blood alcohol limit to drive?

> The legal blood alcohol limit for drivers is **0.05%.** For commercial drivers, it is **0.02%.** *For more details, see Chapter 5.*

Firearm & Ammunition Offenses

Can I possess a gun?

> **No.** Possessing a gun in Costa Rica as a tourist is generally illegal unless you have a special permit.

Can I possess ammunition?

> **No.** You cannot possess ammunition without the proper legal authorization in Costa Rica. *For more details, see Chapter 6.*

Prostitution

Is prostitution legal?

> **Yes.** Prostitution is legal in Costa Rica, but it is regulated. However, pimping or exploitation is illegal, and certain areas have specific laws regarding where it can occur. *For more details, see Chapter 7.*

LGBTQ

Is homosexuality legal?

> **Yes.** Homosexuality is legal in Costa Rica.

Are same-sex public displays of affection legal?

> **Yes.** Same-sex public displays of affection are also legal, though they may not always be widely accepted in all areas, especially more rural regions. *For more details, see Chapter 8.*

Arrested in Costa Rica

Would I be entitled to bail if I'm arrested?

Yes. You may be entitled to bail in Costa Rica, depending on the nature of the offense and the judge's discretion.

Will a lawyer be provided to me if I cannot afford one?

If you cannot afford a lawyer, one may be provided to you, as Costa Rica guarantees the right to legal representation for those unable to pay. *For more details, see Chapter 10.*

Helping a Friend or Relative Imprisoned in Costa Rica

Can I send money to a friend or relative imprisoned in Costa Rica?

Yes. You can send money to a friend or family member imprisoned in Costa Rica, usually through money transfer services or deposits made to their prison account.

Can I remain in Costa Rica upon release from prison or jail after my sentence is complete?

Yes. After completing your sentence, you can remain in Costa Rica, but you may need to ensure your immigration status is in order, as a criminal record could affect your ability to stay legally. *For more details, see Chapter 12.*

Crime Victim Assistance

Can a victim of a crime be legally compensated?

Yes. A victim of a crime in Costa Rica can be legally compensated, particularly in cases of personal injury or property damage, through the judicial system or insurance claims.

Does the Costa Rican government offer assistance for family members of homicide victims?

Yes. The Costa Rican government does offer assistance to family members of homicide victims, including psychological support and compensation through the Victim Support Program under the National Institute of Criminal Defense (INL). *For more details, see Chapter 14.*

U.S. Consulate Assistance

Are there any limitations to the consulate assistance I can receive while in Costa Rica?

Yes. Consulate assistance in Costa Rica has some limitations. Consulates can help with issues like passport replacement, legal referrals, and emergency travel documents, but they cannot provide financial support, settle legal disputes, or interfere in local legal matters. They also cannot offer representation in criminal or civil cases. *For more details, see Chapter 14.*

Police

Is there an official police force?

Yes. Costa Rica has an official police force called the Fuerza Pública (Public Force), which is responsible for maintaining public order, enforcing laws, and protecting citizens. There are also specialized police units, such as the Judicial Investigation Police (OIJ), which handle criminal investigations. *For more details, see Chapter 15.*

How to Get Legal Help in Costa Rica

Is there a resource in Costa Rica to find legal representation?

Yes. In Costa Rica, you can find legal representation through the Costa Rican Bar Association (*Colegio de Abogados y Abogadas de Costa Rica*), which has a directory of licensed lawyers.

Is there free legal representation assistance?

Yes. Free legal representation is available for those who cannot afford it through the Public Defender's Office (Defensoria Publica), which provides legal assistance in criminal, civil, and family law matters for eligible individuals. *For more details, see Chapter 16.*

Foreign Embassies in Costa Rica

Are there foreign embassies in Costa Rica?

Yes. There are foreign embassies in Costa Rica, including those of the United States, Canada, and several European countries.

Is there a website to locate embassies in Costa Rica?

Yes. You can locate embassies in Costa Rica through the official website of the Ministry of Foreign Affairs and Worship of Costa Rica at **https://www.rree.go.cr/**, or by searching for individual embassy websites for more specific information. *For more details, see Chapter 16.*

Medical Facilities & Hospitals

Is there a number I can call for ambulance and fire emergencies?

Yes. For ambulance and fire emergencies in Costa Rica, you can call **911.**

If I am injured while on vacation in Costa Rica, are there hospitals that are recommended for tourists?

Yes. If you are injured while on vacation, recommended hospitals for tourists include Hospital Cima in San José (private hospital with English-speaking staff) and Hospital Clínica Bíblica, which also caters to international patients. Both are well-equipped for emergencies and general healthcare needs. *For more details, see Chapter 17.*

Driving in Costa Rica

Which side of the road do I drive on?

In Costa Rica you drive on the **right-hand side** of the road.

Can I use my driver's license from my home country to drive in Costa Rica?

>Yes. You can use your driver's license from your home country to drive in Costa Rica for up to 90 days as a tourist.

How old do I need to be to rent a car?

>To rent a car in Costa Rica, you typically need to be at least **21 years old**, although some rental agencies may require drivers to be 25 or older. *For more details, see Chapter 18.*

Nude Beaches & Clothing-Optional Resorts

Is public nudity legal on the beaches?

>**No.** Public nudity is not legal on the beaches in Costa Rica. While some remote or secluded beaches may see occasional nudity, it is not officially permitted, and authorities may issue fines or ask individuals to cover up. *For more details, see Chapter 19.*

Tourist Taxation

Is there room tax in Costa Rica?

>**Yes.** There is a room tax in Costa Rica, typically around 13% of the total accommodation cost.

Is there any fee associated with leaving Costa Rica?

>**No.** There is no longer a separate exit fee for leaving Costa Rica; the departure tax is now included in the price of your airline ticket. *For more details, see Chapter 22.*

Long-Term Stays

Do I need to return to my home country to apply for a work permit in Costa Rica?

> **No.** You do not need to return to your home country to apply for a work permit in Costa Rica. You can apply for a work permit while in Costa Rica, but you will need to meet the specific requirements and have a job offer from a Costa Rican employer.

As an American, how long can I stay in Costa Rica without a visa?

> As an American, you can stay in Costa Rica without a visa for **up to 90** days as a tourist. After 90 days, you would need to leave the country or apply for an extension. *For more details, see Chapter 23.*

In the Event of Death

What documents would an embassy need regarding the death of a tourist?

> If a tourist passes away in Costa Rica, the embassy will need the death certificate, passport or ID of the deceased, and contact information for the next of kin. The person reporting the death would also need to provide proof of identity. If applicable, the embassy may request local police reports or other relevant documents. The embassy will assist with repatriation and legal matters, as well as notifying the family. *For more details, see Chapter 25.*

EMERGENCY/IMPORTANT CONTACT NUMBERS IN COSTA RICA

 Please consider putting some of these numbers in your phone prior to traveling to Costa Rica.

Emergency Numbers:

- **Police:** 911
- **Fire:** 911
- **Ambulance:** 911

Other Useful Contacts:

- **General Emergency Services:** 911
- **Tourist Police:** 800-TOURIST (800-868-7478)
- **Coast Guard:** 118
- **Roadside Assistance:** 800-091-9111

Legal Assistance:

- **Costa Rican Bar Association:** +506-2256-1071
- **Legal Aid--Public Defender's Office (Defensoria Pública):** +506-2583-1111

USEFUL SPANISH PHRASES

 While Spanish spoken in Costa Rica is largely understandable to other Spanish speakers, it is not exactly the same as "standard" Spanish, as it has its own distinct dialect with unique pronunciation, vocabulary, and sometimes grammar variations particularly regarding the use of "vos" instead of "tú" in informal situations.

GREETINGS

HI/HELLO – Hola

GOOD MORNING – Buenos días

GOOD AFTERNOON – Buenas tardes

GOOD NIGHT – Buenas noches

GOODBYE – Adiós

MAGIC WORDS

PLEASE – Por favor

THANK YOU – Gracias

YOU'RE WELCOME – De nada

CHEERS! – ¡Salud!

EXCUSE ME – Perdón/disculpe

GETTING AROUND

WHERE IS THE BATHROOM? – ¿Dónde está el baño?

WHAT TIME IS IT? – ¿Qué hora es?

HOW DO I GET TO…? – ¿Cómo llego a…?

WHERE DOES THIS TRAIN/BUS GO? – ¿A dónde va este tren/autobús?

RESTAURANT – Restaurante

HOW MUCH DOES THIS COST? – ¿Cuánto cuesta esto?

TRAIN/METRO STATION – Estación de tren/metro

COMMUNICATION

DO YOU SPEAK ENGLISH? – ¿Habla inglés?

I DO NOT UNDERSTAND – No entiendo

I DON'T SPEAK SPANISH – No hablo español.

I DON'T KNOW – No sé

EMERGENCY

HELP! – ¡Ayuda!

CALL AN AMBULANCE! – ¡Llame una ambulancia!

I NEED A DOCTOR – Necesito un doctor

POLICE – Policía

I'M LOST – Estoy perdido/a

IT'S AN EMERGENCY – Es una emergencia

GLOSSARY

ACQUITTAL: A jury verdict that a criminal defendant is not guilty, or the finding of a judge that the evidence cannot support a conviction.

ADVERSARY PROCEEDING: A lawsuit arising from a controversy that begins with filing a complaint.

AFFIDAVIT: A written statement made under oath.

APPEAL: A request made after a trial court has decided against one party in which the losing party asks a higher court to review the decision for legal error.

ARRAIGNMENT: A proceeding in which a criminal defendant is brought to court, told of the charges, and asked to plead guilty or not guilty.

BAIL: The temporary release of a person from jail when awaiting trial, on condition that a sum of money be lodged or deposited to guarantee an appearance in court.

BARRISTER: A lawyer admitted to plead at the Bar and who may try cases in superior court.

BURDEN OF PROOF: The duty to prove disputed facts.

CAUSE OF ACTION: A legal claim in a civil action.

COMPLAINT: A written statement that begins a civil lawsuit in which the plaintiff details the claims.

CONTRACT: An agreement between two or more persons to do something or to not do something.

CONVICTION: A judgment of guilt against a person charged with a crime.

CUSTOMS DUTY: A tariff or tax imposed on goods when transported across international borders.

COURT LIAISON: A person that coordinates with attorneys to perform administrative duties, such as scheduling witnesses, sharing information with law enforcement, and overseeing the reporting of cases to foreign embassies when applicable.

DAMAGES: Money that a defendant pays to a plaintiff in a civil case if the plaintiff wins.

DEFENDANT: 1) The individual against whom a civil claim is filed; 2) The individual against whom a criminal claim is filed.

FELONY: A serious crime, punishable by more than one year in prison.

MAGISTRATE: A judicial officer of a district court, who conducts initial proceedings in criminal cases, decides criminal misdemeanor cases, conducts many pretrial civil and criminal matters on behalf of district judges, and decides civil cases with the consent of the parties.

MISDEMEANOR: An offense punishable by one year or less in jail.

PLAINTIFF: A person or business that files a formal complaint with the court.

PLEA: In a criminal case, the answer of "guilty," "not guilty," or "no contest" in response to a criminal charge.

SOLICITOR: A lawyer who advises clients, represents them in lower court, and prepares cases for barristers to try in higher courts.

SOVEREIGN IMMUNITY: A legal doctrine by which the sovereign or the state (i.e. government) cannot commit a legal wrong and thus, it is immune from criminal and civil liability and cannot be sued.

STATUTE: A written law passed by a legislative body.

STATUTE OF LIMITATIONS: A statute prescribing a period of limitation to bring certain types of legal actions. If the action is not brought within that time, the person or entity (in a criminal context) is permanently barred from suing in court.

SUBPOENA: A command, issued under court authority, for a witness to appear and to give testimony.

TESTIMONY: Evidence presented orally by witnesses.

VERDICT: The decision of a judge or jury in a case.

WARRANT: Court authorization to conduct a search or to make an arrest.

ACKNOWLEDGMENTS

This book series would never have seen the light of day without the able assistance of the following people:

Kathy Adams, my paralegal for over 22 years, who is the "Best" I've ever worked with during my entire legal career because of her amazing work ethic, organizational skills, and her ability to think outside of the box in unique and creative ways;

Ally Knez-Siddique, a professional writer, and one of my paralegals, whose eye for detail, according to her, is both a blessing and a curse;

Gino Ibanez, my former law clerk, whose exceptional research skills helped move this book series along in its early stages;

Rosa Diaz Graham, my legal assistant who helped with research and word processing at the very beginning of this project;

Shelia Martin, one of my former paralegals, worked diligently on this series of books, even after taking on another job. Her organizational skills are reflected throughout;

Mindy Scarlett, my marketing and publishing "Guru"! Her creativity and vision have no boundaries!

ABOUT THE AUTHOR

Michael L. Moore practices in Orlando, Florida, the city where he spent his formative years. He credits the trauma of having his brother murdered when he was only 10 years old, as the catalyst that drew him into the practice of law.

Moore attended Florida State University, where he was a member of the FSU debate team. Upon graduating, he was awarded a full scholarship to attend the University of Tennessee College of Law, where he was elected President of the Student Bar Association. He further honed his advocacy and public speaking skills by participating in 'moot court' competitions.

After clerking at the Tennessee Attorney General's office while in law school, Moore moved back to Orlando, Florida, to work at the State Attorney's Office as a prosecutor, and where he was fortunate enough to meet the young lady that would eventually become his wife. Moore moved on to working for private law firms, both local and national, and eventually established his own law firm in 1999. He continues to make Orlando his home base.

It was the murder of a close friend and client in Jamaica that caused Moore to realize that books on laws in other countries were few and far between, and he was inspired to create Law of the Land Publishing. Moore launched Law of the Land Publishing to provide a series of guidebooks and a membership site for tourists and business travelers to stay up to date on the laws in each country they travel to, as well as having access to assistance if they run into legal issues.

"My vision is to educate people on what their legal rights are, and how they can access legal assistance, no matter where they have to travel to in the world," said Moore. "As Americans, we have a right to due process, but in some countries, you don't even have the right to access a square meal when incarcerated. My goal is to provide the information needed to stay out of trouble, as well as having access to assistance if trouble finds you."

www.ingramcontent.com/pod-product-compliance
Lightning Source LLC
Chambersburg PA
CBHW070914120626
46546CB00001B/262